Toward a Theory of Economic Growth

With "Reflections on the Economic Growth of Modern Nations"

Simon Kuznets

Harvard University

The Norton Library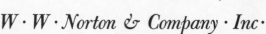

W · W · Norton & Company · Inc ·

New York

Contents

Preface

THE TWO essays reprinted here from *Economic Growth and Structure* (New York: W. W. Norton, 1965) were written in 1953 and 1956. The first presents a broad view of the quantitative analysis of economic growth, while the second summarizes reflections relating largely to non-quantitative aspects of economic growth.

With the passage of time much research has been done in the field, leading to a better perspective. Two conclusions, both in the first essay, need to be specifically noted here as subject to qualification. The first relates to the retardation in the rate of growth of per capita product (see pp. 20–23); the other, to the tendency of major wars to depress economic growth in the participating countries (see pp. 54–57). The first trend is an algebraic necessity in the very long run, but it is less observable and imminent than suggested in the discussion.[1] The second conclusion, while true of the period following World War I, is less clearly applicable to the post-World War II experience,[2] and perhaps should not be asserted as bluntly as it was. Other changes in emphasis could have been made, but they did not seem sufficiently important to warrant revision of the essays, which were written as introductory reviews of a wide field

[1] For a brief summary of evidence see my *Modern Economic Growth* (New Haven: Yale University Press, 1966), Chapter 2, and the more detailed papers cited there.

[2] See my *Postwar Economic Growth: Four Lectures,* (Cambridge: Harvard University Press, 1964), particularly Lecture III.

rather than as definitive statements based on precisely detailed evidence.

Much of the research underlying the papers was based on work initiated under the auspices of the Committee on Economic Growth of the Social Science Research Council. I am indebted to Mrs. Lillian E. Weksler, who assisted me in the original preparation of the papers as well as in reviewing them for republication.

October 1967   SIMON KUZNETS

Toward a Theory of
Economic Growth

THE CURRENT interest in and extensive discussion of the economic growth of nations stem from several sources. A brief review may indicate the major questions that are being raised and point the directions that an approach to a theory may follow.

The Current Interest in Economic Growth

The first recent stimulus was concern over possible secular stagnation in the industrially developed nations. The decline in the rate of population growth of many Western European nations and of European settlements in the New World is not a new phenomenon; it has been commented upon since the late nineteenth century, when the marked and sustained decline in birth rates gave rise to lurid discussion of "race suicide." The reaching of the limits of external expansion, the disappearance of the free frontier, is also an old theme—in fact, an integral element in the economic theory of the long run evolved by the Classical School in the early nineteenth

I am indebted to Professors Moses Abramovitz, John Maurice Clark, Wilbert Moore, and Joseph J. Spengler for many comments made on the first draft of this paper and utilized in revising it.

The discussion draws heavily upon statistical data summarized in an appendix, which has been omitted because of limitations of space.

Reprinted by permission of the Trustees of Columbia University in the City of New York, from Robert Lekachman, ed., National Policy for Economic Welfare at Home and Abroad, Columbia University Bicentennial Conference Series (New York: Doubleday and Company, 1955), pp. 12–85.

century. But the great depression of the 1930's and Keynesian economics, with its emphasis on threatening shortages of private investment opportunities and on their implication in terms of dragging levels of national output and of chronic unemployment, lent new vigor to the stagnation theory. Particularly important, these events served to substitute for the equanimity with which John Stuart Mill, for example, viewed the prospect of a stationary state, a deep anxiety arising from the conviction that secular stagnation meant chronic unemployment and hence a marked failure of the economic system.[1]

With World War II and its aftermath, this concern about economic stagnation receded, but a new source of emphasis on economic growth arose. In its present form this interest is in secular prospects and problems of "underdeveloped" countries, by which we mean countries that have been unable to utilize the opportunities afforded by modern material and social technology and have failed to supply minimum subsistence and material comfort to their populations.[2] This too is no new problem; under-

---

[1] It is instructive to compare Mill's comments in Chapter 5 of Book IV of his *Principles* (in which the stationary state is viewed favorably as relief from the competitive struggle and from overemphasis on material attainments of a "progressive" economy) with the recent anxious discussion in this country of the problem of secular stagnation. True, Mill envisaged the stationary state as operating under a system of greater distributive justice than did the growing state that he and the Classical economists knew, and the policy orientation of modern economists who emphasized the threat of secular stagnation was not unlike Mill's in that they wished to avoid the injustice implied in chronic unemployment. Yet the strong conviction of the indispensability of growth in recent discussion of *industrially advanced* countries is in sharp contrast with Mill's view that "it is only in the backward countries of the world that increased production is still an important object." John Stuart Mill, *Principles,* 5th London ed. (New York: Appleton and Co., 1878), Vol. II, p. 338.

[2] Three definitions of underdevelopment can be suggested. First, it may mean failure to utilize fully the productive potential warranted by the existing state of technical knowledge—a failure resulting from the resistance of social institutions. In this sense, all countries in the world are underdeveloped and have, perhaps, become increasingly so with the rapid growth of technical knowledge during the last century. Second, it may mean backwardness in economic performance, compared with the few economically leading countries of the period. In this sense, the vast majority of countries are underdeveloped at any given time. Third, it may mean economic poverty, in the sense of failure to assure adequate subsistence and material comfort to most of a country's population. The problem of underdeveloped countries in current discussion reflects elements of all three definitions; its acuteness arises largely out of the material misery stressed in the third definition, it is sharpened by realization of a lag compared with other, economically more advanced countries, and it is generally viewed as a social problem originating in the failure of social institutions rather than in a lack of technical knowledge.

developed countries have always been with us. Indeed there is hardly a stretch of human history in which a substantial proportion of mankind has not lagged behind the more advanced communities in utilizing its material potential and therefore experiencing misery and suffering. But the recent emphasis on the problem of economic growth stems from the realization that the nineteenth-century theory of international division of labor, with its promise of the inevitable and rapid spread of the benefits of modern economic civilization to all corners of the earth, is hardly tenable. Further, there is pressure for more rapid economic growth in many underdeveloped countries which, having achieved political freedom recently, are confronted with urgent problems of economic sufficiency and security; and there are increasingly close international ties, which suggest that lack of freedom from want in some countries, with the attendant political and social perturbations, may well mean lack of freedom from fear in others that are economically more advanced.

The third and probably most important reason for the recent interest in economic growth is the emergence of a different social organization which claims greater efficiency in handling long-term economic problems—the authoritarian state of the Soviet type. This offshoot of Western European civilization is again not completely new. Many elements in its organization can be seen, if in rudimentary form, in the histories of Germany and particularly of Japan during periods of rapid industrialization; and, in a sense, the organization of the USSR can be viewed as a further transformation or deformation of the social institutions in the break from the preindustrial to the industrial phase that, for somewhat similar historical reasons, was foreshadowed in German and Japanese experience. On the spiritual side the Soviet case represents ideas and tendencies that have a long history. As I. L. Talmon shows, the roots of "totalitarian democracy" go back to the eighteenth century, and its glorification of the state, controlled by the elect in accordance with a preconceived theory that fits society into a Procrustean bed of some notion of what is good for man, is hardly a new element in Western thought.[3] What is new is the emergence and existence, alongside the economically successful, relatively free democracies, of new authoritarian states whose professed secular religion lies in material achievement and whose theories of orthodoxy and heresy impede free and peaceful intercourse with the rest of the world.

[3] I. L. Talmon, *Origins of Totalitarian Democracy* (London: Secker and Warburg, 1952).

The question immediately raised bears upon the potentialities of such an authoritarian system for the economic growth of both the countries that are and those that are not under its sway.

This recent division of a large part of the world into two camps—both offshoots of the same stream of thought and all the more hostile because of a common belief in the importance of material achievements—lends particular strength to another source of recent interest in economic growth: armed conflict as a major channel of expenditures of economic resources and a powerful accelerator and modifier of long-term trends in the economic and social organization of nations. Here again is an old problem, but the economic aspects have been modified beyond recognition by recent technological and political changes. It is not customary to include wars in discussion of economic growth, and perhaps they should be excluded if a reasonably acceptable theory is to be evolved. But it seems rather dangerous to do so at the start: a substantial proportion of the last two centuries has been accounted for by major wars; preparation for these wars, their conduct, and their aftermaths have significantly transformed long-run economic changes; and armed conflict is to some extent an ultimate expression of the ever-present divisive tendencies among nations.

Can we hope to formulate a theory of economic growth that would indicate the factors in the development of the industrially advanced nations and thus illuminate the problem of possible secular stagnation; to frame the factors so that a testable analysis of obstacles to the economic growth of underdeveloped nations and hence a basis for intelligent development policy become possible; to consider the operation of these factors under a system of free enterprise, as well as within the authoritarian system, so that the potentialities in both and their interplay become clear; and to distinguish the factors that make for peaceful and warlike behavior, so that the bearing of each on economic growth can be perceived? To put the question in this way is to predetermine a negative answer—provided that by a theory we mean a statement of testable relations among empirically identifiable factors, such relations and factors having been found relatively invariant under diverse conditions in time and space. Such a theory of economic growth of nations may never be within our reach. Obviously we do not have it now, and what is more important, we are not yet ready for it. The very concern about economic growth is recent, and it is hardly an exaggeration to say that since the mid-nineteenth century, when the Classical and Marxian Schools had already formulated their economic theories of the long run, no significant theoretical work has been done in this field, excepting the attempts to revise Marxian theory in the light of subsequent events. Meanwhile, with the passage of time, our experience in the economic growth of nations has broadened and empirical records have accumulated, but no significant attempt has been made either to utilize these data within a theoretical framework or ·even to organize, extend, and test them preparatory to theoretical analysis.

These statements are not made as an apology for the limitations of what follows. Nor is it my purpose to provide yet another illustration of the conditions under which economists (and perhaps other social scientists) usually operate—confronted by urgent problems that rapid and complex historical changes bring forth, with no adequate theoretical tools or data for handling them, and under pressure to provide answers in situations in which some intelligence, no matter how limited, is vitally needed. More important in the present context are two implications of the foregoing statements. First, they clearly suggest the need for a long-time and wide-space perspective in the empirical foundation of any theory of economic growth—the body of observations from which it ·must be derived and by which it must be tested. The very understanding of the problems involved, let alone a theoretical formulation and solution, is hardly possible if we limit our view to one country or to a relatively short period of historical experience. Therefore, the following pages summarize the outstanding features of the empirical record of economic growth for a minimum range of time and space.

Second, it is apparent, and will become increasingly striking as we reflect on the variety of growth experience suggested by the empirical evidence, that an explicitly formulated theory of economic growth would at present be of limited usefulness, at least as a tool for research and prediction. Under the present circumstances, such a theory would be either an expression of dogmatic belief in some "self-evident" trait of human nature and corresponding "principle" of social organization; an exercise in the philosophy of history operating with vague terms and elusive units; or a formalistic model of the mechanism of economic growth, lacking assurance that it is complete, that the relations are correctly drawn, and that we can ever have the data required for the empirical constants in the formulas.[4] Interesting as such attempts might be, it seemed preferable to limit ourselves to a less ambitious task: to draw some suggestions from the empirical record about the identity and relative importance of and interconnections among the determining factors, as guides to the further study of the data and particularly to the directions in which testable theoretical analysis must be pursued. In this sense, the title of this paper is truly descriptive; it is *toward* a theory of economic growth that we are attempting to proceed. We may avoid walking off in the wrong direction if we are not required to give explicit answers where no adequate basis for them exists.

Specifications of the Summary

The summary of empirical evidence presented below attempts to bring into view as much of the world as possible, organizes the data around the nation-state as the unit of observation, emphasizes quantitative data, and limits the time range to the last two centuries, although it occasionally forays into earlier times and at many points must, for lack of data, cover a shorter recent period. A brief explanation of these specifications may prevent misunderstanding of the findings.

Statistical data are emphasized because economic growth is essentially a quantitative concept. Much as we are aware, without statistics, of obvious differences in the rate of growth and economic position among the communities that comprise mankind, some notion of the magnitudes is indispensable for clear understanding and analysis. For the purposes of measurement, the economic growth of a nation may be defined as a sustained increase in its population and product per capita.[5] These rates of increase, their pattern over time, and the differential changes of groups within the population

---

[4] This is not meant to deny the value of such hypotheses, nor to claim that it would be possible to forego tools of this type in the immediate future in further organization and analysis of data. All we urge here is the need for a wider view of the phenomena being explored and a recognition of their variability among countries and over time, with proper emphasis on testable empirical evidence.

[5] A combination of secular stagnation or decline of population with a sustained rise in per capita product has been observed only rarely in the last two centuries. Insofar as a definition of economic growth must reflect common experience, it seems best to include a sustained increase in both the total population and the per capita product.

or of components within the product, when compared among nations, are an indispensable record of the basic quantitative aspects of economic growth, of the *results* of the process whose determining factors we would seek to identify in any prospective theory. Sustained movements are those which extend beyond a period so short that they may be confused with transient disturbances, either roughly recurrent and associated with business cycles or more irregular and often associated with calamities, natural or man-made. For practical purposes a period not much shorter than half a century is desirable.

The choice of the nation-state as the unit of observation is partly dictated by the way statistical (and much historical) data, particularly on economic product, are organized; they are ordinarily given for states, largely because states have the power to produce such data and are the foci of interest which these data serve. But there is more here than meets the eye. Modern history suggests that each of these sovereign political units into which mankind is divided identifies a group that claims a distinctive period of common history—a distinct heritage of the past that strongly conditions the process of economic growth—and that the state mechanism, among its many functions, serves as a tool of economic growth, designed to assure the economic security and growth of the society that it organizes. Hence, at least as the first approximate way of ordering the data, there is much to be said for grouping them around the sovereign state as a unit, even though on occasion it may be more convenient to use some larger entities, or at some later stage of analysis it may be concluded that another unit may prove more effective in establishing generalizations.[6]

The limitation to the last two centuries is the result partly of inadequate data for earlier times and partly of the desire to concentrate on a historical period close to us, in which we can more easily orient ourselves. But there are even more fundamental reasons for this choice. The recent centuries subsume all of the human

[6] For a more detailed discussion of this point, see sections contributed by the author to *Problems in the Study of Economic Growth* (National Bureau of Economic Research, July 1949), mimeographed, pp. 3–20 and 118–135, and "The State as a Unit in Study of Economic Growth," *Journal of Economic History*, XI (1951), pp. 25–41.

For larger countries, intracountry regional units may also prove useful since they provide an opportunity to study similarities and differences in growth experience under conditions where cultural and political differences are much narrower than in intercountry comparisons.

past and are a more complete canvas than any earlier period. More specifically, during the last two centuries the potential of economic growth has become particularly large, in both absolute and relative terms; and hence any observable similarities and differences will be of special interest, since they will have developed under conditions more conducive to economic growth than those in the more distant past. Thus, even if data were abundant for, say, the last two centuries B.C., even if we could claim adequate understanding of the material and social conditions of that time, even if we were not concerned with relevance to current problems, we might still argue against that period and for the recent two centuries, largely because, given the state of human knowledge in the earlier period, potentialities for economic growth were narrow and the possible diversity of experience more limited. It is in observing similarities and differences of growth experience where wide diversity is possible that we can form the more tenable notions concerning the factors at play.

Given the choices and emphases just indicated, the effort must be made to bring as much of the world as possible within view. If we are to focus on a period in which potential diversity in rate, pattern, and structure of economic growth is wide, the danger in attempting to generalize from observations for any limited part of the world is all the more obvious. Granted that this goal of a world-wide record is unattainable, particularly for quantitative data, it still should be the desideratum—if only as a goad and as a warning.

We begin the summary with the growth of population, go on to the growth of total and per capita economic product, outline briefly the major changes in the shares of the various components of national product and their implications for the grouping of populations, and conclude with some observations concerning trends in external relations among national units.

Trends in Population Growth

World population increased from about 700 million in 1750 to about 2,400 million in 1950, more than tripling in 200 years. This increase is unusually high when viewed against the known long stretches of human history. The rate of growth from 1750 to 1950 is 6.4 percent per decade, or 85.2 percent per century. If we assume this cumulative rate of growth for the 17.5 centuries between the beginning of the Christian Era (the year 0) and 1750 and start with the 694 million estimated for 1750, the derived world total for year 0 would be about 15,000. Obviously, the rate of growth of world population per century for this period must have been much lower than 85 percent. Indeed, a rough estimate sets world population in year 0 between 200 and 300 million. With 250 million as the base, the average rate of growth per *century* from 0 to 1750 is 6 percent—in sharp contrast with a rate of 85 percent for the last two centuries.[7]

Two aspects of this recent upsurge in population growth deserve note. First, with few exceptions,[8] the increase in population has been widespread, particularly since 1850, by which date the economic and social factors that made it possible began to penetrate to the far corners of the earth. From 1850 to 1950, the population of Asia (excluding the USSR) and Africa almost doubled; of Europe, including Asiatic USSR, more than doubled; of Latin America almost quintupled; of North America more than sextupled. Despite the obvious differences among these continental groups in rates of growth over the last century (they are somewhat more pronounced for the period 1750–1950), the significant fact is that even in the many areas in which current per capita income is quite low, population growth since 1850 has been substantial. On the longer scale of past human history, an increase of 70 to 100 percent over a century is quite high.

Second, the rate of growth of world population has been accelerating. The rate of increase from 1750 to 1850 is 4.6 percent per decade; from 1850 to 1950, 8.2 percent. The rate of growth from 1850 to 1900 is 7.6 percent per decade; from 1900 to 1950, 8.9 percent per decade. This acceleration will not necessarily continue; there is no inevitable law about it. But it does indicate that during recent centuries increasing reservoirs of population growth have been tapped. In considering the implications for the future we must examine the rate of spread of the factors that may explain this recent upsurge in population.

[7] World population by continents is from United Nations, *The Determinants and Consequences of Population Trends* (New York, 1953), Table 2, p. 4. The contrast between the rates of growth is even more striking if we set the dividing point at 1650. On that date, world population is estimated to have been 470 million, and the rate of growth from 1650 to 1750 is 4 percent per decade, much lower than the 6.4 percent for 1750 to 1950 but still much higher than in the earlier period. From the beginning of the Christian Era to 1650 the rate of growth in world population is only 3.9 percent per century, compared with over 72 percent per century for 1650–1950, a ratio of 1 to 18.

[8] See footnote 9.

For this purpose the population-growth experience of individual countries must be taken into account. Although we can hardly do more here than skim the surface, even the most general impressions are important, since individual countries are the proper units of observation and the similarities and differences in their experiences are most revealing.

First, there is a marked diversity in the rates of growth of individual countries. True, for most of them, population grew at much higher rates during the recent century or two than in the long stretches of their historical past.[9] But the rates of growth were substantially different. The differences between the older and the younger countries are hardly surprising: the rate of population increase during the last century in North America was about three times as high as in Europe. The interesting and revealing findings are the differences among countries that are similar in size, age, and many cultural characteristics. Between 1800 and 1900 the rate of growth of population in Sweden was 8.1 percent per decade; in Norway, 9.8 percent; in Denmark, 10 percent; in Finland, 12.2 percent.[10] The differences in the decade rates look small; but they mean that over a century while Sweden's population little more than doubled, Finland's more than tripled.

The records of individual countries also reveal substantial differences in the patterns of growth over time. World population as a whole shows an accelerating rise beginning in the seventeenth century, and, in broad terms, continuing through recent decades. Among individual countries, there are differences in the *timing* of the upward swing in rates of population growth, depending largely upon the population position of the country and the time

[9] Three types of exceptions may be suggested. One, exemplified by Ireland and China since the mid-nineteenth century, represents a sharp break in population growth, leading to a decline or stagnation in total numbers. Another, of which France is an example, represents a late stage in population growth, a phase of retardation yielding rates distinctly below those of some earlier long periods of vigorous growth. A third, comprising the "young," originally relatively "empty" countries of the New World, may not show within the recent centuries *percentage* rates of growth higher than in earlier times, because in these earlier times the bases to which the percentages are calculated are so low. This last group constitutes an exception in a formal rather than substantive sense; and if the comparison were extended far enough back to cover long periods of slow growth in the aboriginal population, it might no longer be an exception.

[10] Underlying data are from R. R. Kuczynski, "Population," in the *Encyclopaedia of the Social Sciences* (New York: Columbia University Press), Vol. 12, pp. 243–245.

when the factors of increased growth came into play. There are also the obvious differences in the time pattern of rates between the young and initially "empty" countries and the older and more densely populated countries. In the former, a high rate of natural increase and substantial immigration made for a high rate of growth in early history; and then, with natural increase and immigration slackening, the rate of growth began to decline long before the recent decades. Thus, in the United States, the rate of increase per decade, adjusted for changes in area, ranges from 33 to 35 percent between 1790 and 1860 and drops to 20 percent or less beginning in 1890.[11] One gets the impression of a truncated swing in the rate of population increase, with the retardation phase quite prominent but the acceleration phase not clearly perceived unless one goes further back in time. In the older countries (mostly in Europe) for which records are sufficiently long, one can observe both the rising and the declining phases in the long swing in rates of population growth. Thus for Europe as a whole, including Asiatic USSR, the increase per decade is 3.4 percent for 1650–1750; 6 percent for 1750–1800; 7.3 percent for 1800–1850; 9.1 percent for 1850–1900; but then it declines to 7 percent for 1900–1950. Finally, in a third group of countries the rate of population growth has not yet begun to decline. The population of Brazil, for example, increased 131 percent from 1840 to 1890 and 190 percent from 1890 to 1940[12]; in several other countries in Latin America and Asia the rate of population growth has been accelerating within recent decades. This variety of time patterns in the rate of growth for individual countries reveals that a sustained acceleration in the rate of increase of world population is not typical of most countries but is due to the successive entries of additional parts of the world into the orbit of the modern population growth pattern.

In considering the forces that made for both the rapid growth of world population and the diverse experience of individual countries during the recent two centuries, we first note the immediate determinants. For world population they are the crude birth and death rates, the excess of the former over the latter yielding the rate of increase in number. For individual countries there are in addition the rates of immigration and emigration. Although these rates are in a sense components of total change rather than causa-

[11] See Walter F. Willcox, *International Migrations* (New York: National Bureau of Economic Research, 1931), Vol. II, p. 98.

[12] From *The Determinants and Consequences of Population Trends*, p. 15.

tive factors, they reflect distinct substantive groups of actions and provide direct leads to the underlying forces at play.

Despite the inadequacies of data and analysis, the connection between the immediate determinants—birth and death rates—and the accelerated rate of increase of world population in recent centuries can be easily summarized.

1. The rise in the rate of population growth was due largely to the reduction in the death rate, *not* to any increase in the birth rate. True, in those countries where the medieval organization inhibited early marriages, birth rates increased for a while as guild and agricultural tenancy restrictions were relaxed and as new industries grew apace. Also, with the changing geographic distribution of world population, the world birth rate (a weighted average) may have risen because of a shift toward more prolific groups. But these are minor qualifications and for the recent century are more than offset by the *decline* in the birth rate in many countries.

Premodern death rates were well above 25 per 1,000 annually in "normal," nonepidemic, nonfamine, nonwar years; and birth rates were ordinarily somewhat above 30 per 1,000. However, the gap (i.e., the rate of natural increase) was much narrower than about 5 per 1,000, as suggested by these figures, because of epidemics, famines, and wars: only 0.6 per 1,000 per year since the rate of increase in population per *century* was about 6 percent. In the advanced countries the death rate has fallen to 10 or less per 1,000. The birth rate has not risen during any period within the last two centuries more than 2 or 3 points above the premodern level and recently declined in the more advanced countries to between 15 and 20 per 1,000.

It is particularly important to note that for centuries mankind lived under conditions in which deaths could easily outpace births. Annual crude birth rates have a fairly low biological ceiling, well below 100 per 1,000 (actually observed rates of as high as 50 are quite rare) because women in childbearing ages can constitute only a limited fraction of any normal population, because the number of children these women can bear during a year is limited by natural laws that govern the number of single and multiple births, and because the total number of children born to a woman is invariably fewer than the number of years in her childbearing period. Annual crude death rates can be much higher, as numerous experiences during earlier centuries indicate, and not only during years of plague or famine. It is the success of modern material and social technology in lowering death rates that has improved so markedly the conditions of population growth that characterized human history for centuries.

2. The forms of the reduction in the death rate are of particular bearing upon economic growth. The age-specific mortality curve is U shaped, with very high rates at the two ends—the infant and very young ages and the more advanced ages past 50. The decrease has been particularly large in the rates at infant and preadult ages, with the result that the enormous waste of breeding children who never reach productive ages has been reduced and the ratio of working-age groups to total population has increased. Furthermore, the factors that make for a decline in deaths have gradually become effective in controlling epidemics and thus have curbed the incidence of the major uncertainties of human life, with possible important effects on the time horizon of individual and social planning. Also, the improvements in medical practice and material conditions of life must have curbed the incidence of nonfatal disease and thus markedly reduced economic losses associated with the latter. Finally, greater control over the death rate meant, even if with some lag, greater control over health conditions in large and densely settled human aggregates, and made the modern large cities possible without catastrophic drains through increased death incidence. Before modern times, death rates were much higher in the cities than in the countryside; this difference was wiped out by the increased knowledge and advanced technology that made for the over-all reduction in mortality.

3. If birth rates had declined as rapidly as death rates, there would have been no acceleration in the growth of world population. In fact birth rates remained constant or declined, either with a lag after the decline in death rates or at a significantly lower rate. This lag and the lesser rate of decline in birth rates were due, at least in part, to the slowness with which population either was subjected or reacted to changing conditions of social life. Slowness is, of course, a relative concept. In other words, changes in medical arts, public health measures, and the standard of living could, at least for a long while, act more rapidly and effectively on the death rates than any modification of social conditions could on the birth-rate habits that had such a long history.

That the lag and disparity are necessarily temporary is revealed by the experience of countries that entered the modern phase of population growth early and where the process had a longer time to develop. In these countries, mostly in Western Europe (disregarding the New World where immigration played an important part), the decline in birth rates began to outpace that in death rates in the 1890's. Since the lower limit to crude death rates is significantly above 0—all people must die some time—rates of less than 10 per 1,000 leave a narrow absolute margin for further reduction. If at the same time birth rates are about 20 per 1,000, the absolute reduction in birth rates can easily exceed that in death rates. The position during the 1890's was somewhat different, with birth rates at 30 and death rates at 20 per 1,000; but by halving both birth and death rates the rate of natural increase is reduced from 10 to 5 per 1,000.

Against this oversimplified but roughly valid picture of major movements in birth and death rates that account for the amazing growth of world population in recent centuries, the records of individual countries suggest a bewildering variety of combinations of immediate determinants. In addition to births and deaths, we must consider here emigration and immigration—flows of considerable importance in both the European countries and the areas of the New World into which the migrants moved—from the eighteenth century until the recent restrictions. We must also consider the chronology of the movement of the death rates and birth rates, the levels at which the declines in both begin, and the magnitude and timing of these declines, all of which differ so much from country to country. The movements are of course similar in that, as time passes, one country after another adopts the modern population growth pattern, with its decline in death rates, eventual decline in birth rates, and replacement of violent temporal fluctuations by a steadier course free from the impacts of epidemics and famines. Yet there still are marked differences among countries in their initial positions and in the subsequent combinations of the immediate determinants of birth, death, and migration; and it is these differences that should be the important raw material for analyses leading to a theory of economic growth.

For any given historical period, the population growth of a given country is arithmetically determined by the initial levels of its crude birth, death, and external migration rates, the timing as well as the magnitude of the declines in birth and death rates, and the course of the rate of external migration. There is room here for a variety of combinations productive of a great diversity of average rates of population growth, as well as of the pattern of such growth over time—let alone of different impacts upon the sex and age structure of the population, which have further consequences for economic growth. High birth and death rates may continue for the larger part of a historical period and be affected by factors making for declines only toward the end; yet, if combined with some net immigration, the result may be a high rate of total population growth. On the other hand, birth and death rates may decline rapidly, with the rate of natural increase also declining; but if the rate of immigration is rising, a high rate of population increase may be sustained. There is the case, typical of many older European countries, where fairly early in the modern period death and birth rates were already somewhat lower than they are today in many underdeveloped countries; where the rate of natural increase accelerated because of a rapid decline in death rates and a lag in the decline of birth rates; but where the overall increase was limited by substantial losses through emigration.

A complete typology of countries for the last two centuries, or even the last century—dividing them by groups with distinctive combinations of levels and movements of birth, death, and migration rates—is impossible here. Indeed, judging by the discussion in the United Nations, *The Determinants and Consequences of Population Trends,* such an attempt would be extremely difficult even for a demographic expert, partly because of scarcity of basic data and partly because of great lacunae in the analysis of data already available, which would have to be studied systematically country by country for long periods of recent history. We can only point to the obvious variety of population growth experience, even among countries that are not too different with respect to size and character of economic and social institutions, and emphasize that such differences are relevant to the similarities and differences in economic growth. Birth, death, and migration rates have a direct impact on the absolute number of population, on its sex and age structure and the consequent ratio of producers to dependents, on the adaptability of the labor force connected with accession of the younger generations and retirement or migration of the older, on the general processes of internal mobility caused by disparities between the differential rates of natural increase and the rate of increase of economic and other opportunities. More elusive, but perhaps even more important, is the indirect association between population growth patterns and economic growth, through the impress that stability (or instability) of human life and freedom (or lack of freedom) to migrate put upon the whole economic and social order. One may assume that the premodern population movement, characterized by high birth and death rates, probably limited the time horizon of an individual and resulted in a pattern of family organization, cultural response, and social ideology which could hardly favor the individual self-reliance that was such an important factor in economic growth during the past two centuries, or at least before World War I. Likewise, the possibilities of gains and losses through free migration, the freedom with which groups in the prime of their working life can move to countries offering better opportunity, create conditions that, however they threaten the countries of origin with direct loss, may benefit even them in the long run, as they do the recipient countries. It is this variety of interconnections between population and economic growth that makes it difficult to envisage an adequate theory of economic growth as long as the record and analysis of the diverse population experience of the countries of the world are so incomplete.

Trends in the Growth of National Product

Among the most effective measures of the economic performance of a nation is its total net product, or national income—the sum of all goods produced during a given period, adjusted for duplication, and net of any commodities consumed in the process of production. If available for a long period, measured in constant prices, and accompanied by estimates of significant components, such measures provide an invaluable picture of the broader aspects of a nation's economic growth. But even disregarding questions of detail that concern components, estimates of national income for a period sufficiently long to permit observation of growth, and acceptable even by lenient standards of statistical reliability, are now available for only fourteen countries, almost all economically developed and with high per capita income. For recent years, however, we have estimates for some 70 to 75 countries. Although many are exceedingly crude, these current estimates, combined with the few available for long periods, can yield a basis for some reasonable inferences about national income trends over the last century.

CHANGES IN PER CAPITA INCOME · Of the 2 billion people in the countries for which estimates of national income were available for

1949, over 30 percent had per capita income of less than $50, and almost one quarter more, between $50 and $100. These were countries in Asia, Africa, the Middle East, and Central and South America. At the other extreme were the United States, the United Kingdom, the Scandinavian countries, Switzerland, Canada, Australia, and New Zealand, which together accounted for 11 percent of the population covered and in which per capita income was $600 or more. The 400 million for whom no national income estimates are available would be mostly in the lower income brackets. One may, therefore, conclude that more than 60 percent of the world's population had per capita incomes of $100 or less; that less than 10 percent had per capita incomes of $600 or more; and that the rest ranged in a spectrum with the older Western European countries at the upper end and several Latin American countries and Japan at the lower end.[13]

As the compilers themselves recognize, such per capita income estimates tend to understate the economic levels of the less developed countries if only because the large volume of nonmarket-bound activities may be inadequately covered. There are many other reasons, whose exploration is out of place here, why statistical comparisons of this type tend to exaggerate the contrast between industrially advanced and underdeveloped countries.[14] But even if we make generous allowances for biases, striking differences in per capita income remain. Granted that the true ratio of per capita income in the United States to that in China is not 54 to 1, as the United Nations figures indicate, but only 10 or 15 to 1, this difference is still large. Such a large gap in per capita income must mean vast differences in the structure of the productive apparatus of the countries, in the extent to which they have adopted modern economic and social technology, in the health, education, and urbanization of their populations, and indeed in the whole set of social values. Manipulation of figures too often obscures the fact (and not only to statisticians) that differences in quantities,

[13] Underlying data are from W. S. and E. S. Woytinsky, *World Population and Production* (New York: Twentieth Century Fund, 1953), Table 185, pp. 389–390; and United Nations, Statistical Papers, Series E, No. 1 (New York, 1950), entitled *National and Per Capita Incomes, Seventy Countries, 1949*, Tables 1 and 4.

[14] See "National Income and Industrial Structure," *Proceedings of the International Statistical Conferences 1947* (Calcutta, 1951), Vol. V, pp. 205–239; reprinted in Simon Kuznets, *Economic Change* (New York: W. W. Norton and Co., 1953).

once they pass beyond a certain range, are symptomatic of cardinal differences in quality, an observation that should be kept in mind also in considering changes over time.

Our long records of national income are with some exceptions (Italy, Japan) for countries at the top of the income pyramid. The rates of growth in per capita income range mostly from about 10 percent to over 20 percent per decade. These rates are extremely high; an increase of 10 percent per decade means a rise over a century to over 2.5 times the initial value; and an increase of 20 percent means a rise over a century to more than 6 times the initial value. In fact, the rise per century in per capita income varied, for the countries for which we have fairly long records, from about 2.5 times (in France and the United Kingdom) to over 7 (in Sweden, and excluding the exceptionally high but statistically dubious rate for Japan between the 1870's and World War II).[15] Here again biases in statistical estimation tend to undervalue earlier periods compared with more recent ones and thus exaggerate the rate of growth. These biases, however, are less pronounced than those in cross-section comparisons among developed and underdeveloped countries. And again, even if we allow for the biases, the rises are sufficiently large to signify major changes in the underlying organization of life.

From the evidence relating to the international comparisons for 1949 and the limited number of long-term records on total and per capita income, several tentative inferences can be drawn. First, the *current* income levels in many countries with less than $100 per capita income are desperately low—low to a point where the means of subsistence are hardly adequate. In these countries, the per capita income could not have grown much over the last hundred years, since this would imply incomes too low at the beginning of the century to allow the population to survive, particularly since an insufficient quantity of goods could not be offset as well then as today by sanitary and medical controls. In China, India, Indonesia, Indochina, most of the Middle East, Africa, and many parts of Latin America, the population could hardly survive on half or perhaps even three quarters of current income levels. Yet we know that population has increased in almost all of them, in many substantially. It follows that if any secular rise in per capita

[15] See the author's "Quantitative Aspects of the Economic Growth of Nations: I. Levels and Variability of Rates of Growth," *Economic Development and Cultural Change*, V, 1 (October 1956), Tables 1 and 2.

income did take place in these countries over the last century, it must have been much smaller than the rise observed among the developed countries.

Second, for most of the *older* countries in this category (excluding some Latin American countries, Java under Dutch rule, Egypt in recent decades), population growth over the last century, while substantial, was at an appreciably lower rate than in countries that enjoyed a rapidly rising per capita income. It follows that growth of *total* national income, in constant prices, during the last century was also at a much lower rate in most currently underdeveloped countries than in countries now in the upper levels of the income pyramid. Third, since the countries with currently high per capita income (with some exceptions such as Japan) displayed the high rates of growth in per capita income during the last century, one hundred years ago international differences in per capita income must have been narrower, certainly absolutely and probably relatively, than they are today.

A fourth inference, somewhat less firm than the other three, can be drawn concerning per capita income levels in underdeveloped countries today compared with those in the developed countries before their industrialization. The current contrast between underdeveloped and more advanced countries appears to result only in part from differences in the rates of growth in per capita income during the last century; part results from differentials already existing in earlier days. This conclusion is suggested first by the contrast between the range of rates of growth in per capita income and the range of present *cross-section* differences in per capita income. Thus, for purposes of illustration, let us assume that the per capita incomes of China and Sweden are currently in the ratio of 1 to 10. A hundred years ago, well before the industrialization of Sweden began, Swedish per capita income, which grew faster than that in almost any other Western country, was about a seventh of its present level. If the per capita income of China had been the same a hundred years ago as it is today, it follows that even in 1850, well before Sweden entered its period of industrialization, per capita income was at least 1.4 compared with 1 in China; and if there has been any increase in the per capita income of China, the ratio was higher. Some corroboration of this inference is provided by Colin Clark's crude figures. His estimates of international units per worker for the presently developed countries, at the time before their industrialization—Great Britain in 1800 or even 1688, the United States in 1830, Sweden in the 1860's, Germany in 1854, Belgium in 1854, France in the 1840's—are all above 300. The same measure is 138 for China in 1935; 230 to 250 for British India in the 1930's and the 1940's; 153 for Brazil in 1928, but rising rapidly to 297 in 1946; 100 for Japan in 1887, and only 190 as late as 1920.[16]

If per capita income in many parts of the world is today significantly lower than it was in the currently developed countries before their industrialization, some fascinating questions arise upon which our data shed no light at all. Before the nineteenth century, and perhaps not much before it, some presently underdeveloped countries, notably China and parts of India, were believed by Europeans to be more highly developed than Europe, and at that earlier time their per capita incomes may have been higher than the then current incomes of the presently developed countries. If so, per capita income in these original economic leaders, now underdeveloped countries, declined substantially or, what is more likely, per capita income of the European countries and their settlements overseas rose substantially *before* industrialization. These speculations point up the need for an analysis of the phases of growth in developed countries before their industrialization and for information on the effects for many underdeveloped countries of today of the heritage of past economic superiority in the way of a large population and a social mechanism which, however effective in the past, and perhaps *because* it was so effective, has become obsolete and now constitutes a serious obstacle to the adoption of modern economic and social technology.

Turning now to the pattern of change over time revealed by the long period estimates of national income (and population), mostly for the economically advanced countries proper, we observe in most a *retardation* in the rate of growth of population, total income, and per capita income. If we could follow the historical record back far enough, we should find in all countries a period of *acceleration* in the rate of growth: in the older and already settled countries, such as the United Kingdom, in population, total income, and income per capita, since the high rate of growth of population and income per capita are modern phenomena and in fact were initiated within the two centuries under review; in the younger and initially "empty" countries, such as the United States, Canada, and Australia, in per capita income but not neces-

---

[16] The figures are from Colin Clark, *Conditions of Economic Progress*, 2d ed. (London, 1951).

sarily in population and total income, since their rates of population growth may have been high from the very beginning. The picture thus suggested for countries that were well settled by 1750 is that of a long swing from low rates of growth in population, total income, and per capita income to much higher ones, then to declining rates. For countries that were relatively empty at the beginning of the period, we observe a truncated swing of rates of growth in population and perhaps, although less likely, in total income, with high rates at the very beginning, then lower ones; and a complete swing in the rates of growth of per capita income, with low rates of growth, succeeded by higher rates as industrialization begins, then followed by retardation.

The statistical records for delineating the periods of growth before industrialization are quite scanty. There is a suggestion (in the record of the United States before 1840, of Sweden before the 1880's, even of Great Britain before the 1820's) that the acceleration in the rate of growth of population is initiated before that in growth of per capita income: the swarming of population, to use the demographers' term, is such that despite the technological changes the rise in total income can barely keep up with or only slightly exceeds the increase in numbers. It is only with some lag, as the high rate of population growth becomes stabilized or begins to decline and as the process of industrialization gets into full swing, that a significant increase in the rate of growth of per capita income is attained. This early phase, rapid rates of growth of population and total income but not of per capita income, is in many ways crucial. To this phase belong the early shifts in structure of the economy, away from agriculture and toward industry. It is in this phase that rapid adjustments must be made to the changing conditions constituted by the differential impact on the several classes of population swarming and of the technological changes made possible by the same factor that made for larger numbers. It is, therefore, in this phase that many "secular" decisions are made that have a lasting effect on the rate, pattern, and character of economic growth unfolded through the later decades.

Although no statistical analysis of this phase is presently possible, historical records indicate an important aspect of economic growth. This early phase of transition to the modern industrial economy is characterized by great internal strains and conflicts, consequences of the shifts in relative economic position and power of various groups affected differently by the increases in numbers and by the opportunities of the new technology. These accelerations of the rate of growth of population and total income appear, when viewed statistically, as rather placid movements of steadily climbing lines. But under the surface there are major shifts among social groups, some of which will be touched upon in the next sections; and the very change in the rate of increase over time may involve serious strains on the pre-existing framework of society geared to a much slower rate of growth. Historical records of this phase, which we cannot date exactly—about 1780 to 1820 in Great Britain, 1810 to 1860 in the United States, 1820 to 1870 in Germany—reveal the many conflicts and strains, even to the point of bringing on a civil war (as in this country). They also reveal the scores of basic secular decisions and adjustments that were made on land tenure, immigration and emigration, the disposition of land in the public domain, the treatment of industry with respect to subsidies and tariffs, the relation of government to the necessary internal improvements, and the like. These adjustments and decisions are clearly important in their effects on the economic growth that followed; the presence of these strains and conflicts, and their resolution, as the concomitant of the changes in rate of growth, must be kept in view. By doing so we can avoid treating the statistical trend lines as mysteriously inevitable paths. If conflicts and strains arose and secular decisions had to be made, the implication is that there were several possible decisions, and that the choice of one, explicable perhaps in terms of a variety of conditions, was not inevitable in the sense that feasible changes in such a decision could not have substantially modified the outcome.

This observation can be repeated about the deceleration phase in the growth of the over-all totals of population, income, and per capita income observed in many industrially advanced countries. A decline in the rate of growth is inevitable only as an abstraction, in the bromidic sense that nothing can grow forever, but forever is a long time and permits unretarded growth for thousands of years. If retardation is observed within decades, it can hardly be interpreted as inevitable; it must be due to specific historical circumstances. Because they were specific, arising out of particular constellations of historical factors, they left room for alternative decisions in the sense that at any given time a different combination of factors, either as to identity or weight, was possible. As later discussion suggests, one important factor in retardation within the historically observed period was the organization of the world into separate sovereign units and the recurring transformation of international competition into armed conflict. In this light, the slowly retarding trend lines of the statistical record are not inevitable in the sense that they will run their full course along set paths. There are serious breaks in many of the records—for Germany, Japan, Russia, and Austria, among others. Thus both internal and external strains and conflicts are an almost continuous accompaniment of the process of growth which, when viewed statistically, appears so consistent and steady for long periods. One of the most difficult and intriguing tasks of a theory of economic growth is to combine both the disruptive and the integrative, the qualitatively changing and the quantitatively steady, aspects of the process.

Shifts in Industrial Structure

The component structures of a nation's aggregate product or income that are ordinarily distinguished include: (1) the industrial sectors in which product originates; (2) the income streams—wages, salaries, entrepreneurial income, dividends, interest, and so forth—that flow to the several productive factors engaged (labor, property, enterprise); (3) the origin of income in economic entities with different forms of organization—individual firms, ordinary business corporations, public utility corporations, nonbusiness corporations, and governments; (4) the allocation of income payments among recipients grouped either by the size of income or according to institutionally distinguishable social groups; (5) the distribution of national income, viewed as congeries of final products, between flow into consumption and capital formation, with numerous categories within each of these two main components; (6) the distinction between products originating and retained at home and the inflows and outflows across the nation's boundaries. An adequate study of even the quantitative aspects of economic growth requires consideration of all these component structures for as many countries and for as long a period within the last two centuries as data permit. Lack of space and particularly scarcity of data prevent such full treatment. We limit our brief discussion to two main distributions: by industrial origin and between flow into consumption and capital formation.

Changes or differences in the industrial structure of economies can be studied through the distribution of the labor force, capital, and income originating. Of these it is the first for which the richest stock of data is available and the one for which conceptual difficulties are least formidable. Data on capital by industrial categories are quite scanty. Although information on the industrial distribution of national income is more plentiful, the derivation of totals in *constant* prices is beset with difficulties. The adjustment for price changes, when we try to estimate *net* income originating in the several industrial sectors, must take account either of their differing cost structures and differential changes in prices affecting the elements of cost payments to other industries and gross product, or of the different living conditions of people attached to the several industries and hence the different levels and trends in the purchasing power of the money incomes they receive. It is, therefore, most practicable to summarize shifts in industrial structure primarily in terms of changing distributions of the labor force, with only secondary reference to changes in the industrial distribution of national income.[17]

THE SHIFT AWAY FROM AGRICULTURE · Because the trends are similar and cross-section differences well established, the summary can be brief.[18] First, in the countries where per capita income grew significantly, the proportion of the labor force engaged in agriculture declined and that engaged in nonagricultural industries increased. The shifts have been quite marked. Thus in the United States the share of the labor force in agriculture was over 70 percent in 1820 and less than 20 percent in 1940. In Japan, this share was 72 percent in 1870 and less than 30 percent by the mid-1930's. Second, in comparing the industrial structure of countries at a recent date, we find a close negative association between per capita income and the share of the labor force in agriculture: the higher the former, the lower the latter, and vice versa. Thus, the share of the labor force in agriculture in India, China, Indonesia, and many of the poorer countries in Latin America is between 60 and 70 percent; that in countries with high income per capita, even

[17] We should note, however, some of the limitations of analysis based upon the labor force. These data reflect only part of the input, neglect quality differences among various groups, including those due to training, and do not ordinarily record changes in hours. But they are adequate for the broad picture sought here, and are particularly illuminating for the changes in the whole mode of life of the population associated with changing industrial structure.

[18] Underlying data are largely from Clark, *op. cit.*

those that are great exporters of agricultural products (Canada, Australia, New Zealand), is usually well below 30 percent. Third, since the share of the labor force in agriculture in the under-developed countries is so high today, it could not have been much higher in the past: if it is 70 percent now, its absolute decline over the past century could not have begun to approach the decline of 50 percentage points in the United States. It follows that there must have been an association between the moderate rise (if any) over the last century in per capita income of the presently under-developed countries and the moderate decline (if any) in the share of labor in agriculture. Fourth, product per worker in agriculture is generally lower than in all nonagricultural industries combined, and its rate of growth is not as high as that in many nonagricultural industries such as mining, manufacturing, trans-portation, and communication utilities. It follows that the share of agriculture in national income is generally lower than its share in the labor force, and that over the long run, its share in national income may have declined more than its share in the labor force. This inference, however, should be qualified because of difficulties involved in imputation of the net income of industries in constant prices, and because of questions relating to long-term trends in product per worker in most service industries.

For the more advanced countries, in which nonagricultural indus-tries grew to dominate the labor force and the product, we should also note some significant trends in the distribution of the non-agricultural sectors proper. The shares of mining and manufacturing in the total labor force grew significantly, but the increases have ceased or slowed down during recent decades. The shares of the transportation and communication industries in the labor force also grew but became stable after World War I or even before; yet they never reached sizable proportions because of the extremely high capital intensity and product per worker and the remarkably high rate of growth in per worker product. The shares of trade and other service industries, a miscellaneous group including business, personal, professional, and government services, have grown stead-ily and have continued to grow in recent decades. The distribution in the United States in 1940 shows less than 20 percent of the labor force in agriculture; somewhat over 30 percent in mining, manu-facturing, and construction, primarily in manufacturing; only 6 per-cent in transportation and communication; and about 43 percent in trade and other services. In general, trends in the nonagricultural sectors' shares in national income followed the trends in their shares in the labor force, except for the greater rise in productivity per worker in such technologically advanced sectors as mining, manufacturing, and the public utilities. It is, of course, in dealing with net product, in constant prices, originating in the service industries, that the conceptual difficulties in estimation are at their perplexing worst.

This capsule summary contains little that is unfamiliar. The shift away from agriculture is perhaps best known and has led to the widespread identification of modern economic growth with industrialization, by which is usually meant the growing absolute and relative volume of industry as contrasted with agriculture. The causes, implications, and corollaries of these shifts in industrial structure are also for the most part familiar. But we mention them briefly, with primary emphasis on the shift from the agricultural sector to the nonagricultural sectors and on the interrelations of the implications and corollaries of the shifts.

If in country A the share of agriculture in the labor force declines from 70 to 20 percent while per capita income increases significantly, and if, to simplify the argument, we assume a constant ratio of population to the labor force (say 2.5 to 1) and no international trade, the trend means that each group of 250 in total population was supplied at the end of the period by only 20 workers in agriculture instead of the original 70. How could such a change be attained? There are two possibilities: (1) Despite the increase in income or consumption per capita, population used a lower *absolute* per capita volume of products of agricultural labor. This may have been due to either (*a*) substitution or (*b*) absolute reduction in per capita use, without substitution. (2) The rate of increase in per worker productivity in agriculture may have been higher than the rate of expansion of per capita demand for agricultural products. With such a differential, the ratio of agricultural workers to total population would drop; under the assumption of a constant ratio of population to labor force, the ratio of agricultural workers to all workers would also decline. If we now assume that the country engages in international trade, we introduce a third implication: (3) It may have reduced the share of exports in the total product of agriculture or increased the share of imports in the total use of agricultural products.

Implication (1*b*) is unrealistic and can be rejected: countries with rising income and rising consumption per capita do not reduce per capita use of the aggregate product of agriculture. Implication (3), however relevant in dealing with the economic growth of any one country, is of limited usefulness on a world-wide scale. With no absolute reduction in world-wide per capita use of agricultural products and the prevalence of declines in the share of agriculture in the labor force, reduced exports or increased imports of agricultural products of country A only shift the question to countries B, C, D, and so forth. How can these countries adjust to decreased imports from or increased exports to country A, while their own per capita use of agricultural products does not decline and agriculture's share in labor does? This is not to deny that international division of labor in agriculture (and in other sectors) and shifts in it are not important in the study of economic growth. The only point here is that it cannot be used (without additional considerations concerning shifts of weights in many world-wide totals, which cannot be pursued here) to explain trends in the distribution of the labor force and product away from agriculture, observed in so many countries and not offset by opposite movements in any. Under these conditions, only implications (1a) and (2) are relevant.

Examining them against the historical background of an advanced country, we find that both explanations are important. The substitution for products of agricultural labor assumes two forms. First, direct replacement results from technological changes and changes in taste: when firewood, a farmer's product, is replaced by coal, a product of nonagricultural labor, the case is clear, as are the cases of cotton being replaced by nylon and some foodstuffs by vitamin pills. Second, there is substitution only in the sense of a shift in the *locus*, not necessarily the nature, of the service. When 70 percent of the labor force, and of the population, was attached to agriculture, it performed many services in addition to agricultural cultivation—baking, spinning, soapmaking, and building—both as a family unit and in cooperation with neighbors. Such services, even if rendered in this fashion, would be classified as the product of agricultural labor. In fact, most of them have now been commercialized, and before they were commercialized few were covered in our national income estimates. The point to be noted is that labor attached to agriculture turns out something in addition to agricultural products, and substitution for the latter is a shift of place, not of product.

But implication (2) is far more important: the combination of a high rate of growth of productivity per worker in agriculture with a lower rate of growth in the per capita use of agricultural products. The former is largely a result of major technological changes, based on growth of tested knowledge and made possible by a proper social adjustment. The latter is partly the result of substitution just noted, partly the result of the basic structure of human wants in which, even in the long run, the need for agricultural products is satiated sooner than the need for nonagricultural products; and partly the result of the changes in mode of life and character of economic and social organization that are corollaries of this shift away from agriculture—urbanization and a more elaborate economic and social structure.

It seems clear that the marked shifts in the structure of the labor force and national product away from agriculture imply not only an industrial revolution, in the sense of major technological changes that provide the basis for increasingly effective use of resources in the nonagricultural sectors, but also an agricultural revolution, in the sense of marked changes in the technology and form of organization of agriculture itself. True, during the period under discussion, thanks to the new revolutionary means of transportation and communication, the expansion of agricultural civilization to hitherto unused, relatively empty areas added to world agricultural production and to agricultural product per worker— an addition that might have occurred even without revolutionary changes in agricultural technology. But since the latter took place in some older countries even before extensive expansion of agriculture to new lands, and since agricultural product per worker in all countries that showed a rise in income per capita also displayed a marked upward trend, changes in agricultural technology and organization must have been largely responsible for and permitted the shift of the labor force and income structure away from agriculture. The rather obvious fact that industrialization supplies a new technological base for *both* agriculture and industry is to be stressed, if only because some recent statistical manipulations of product per worker in agriculture and in other sectors suggest that economic growth is just a matter of easy transfer of labor from "backward" agriculture io "progressive" industry. At the cost of repeating the obvious, it must be stressed that a technological revolution in agriculture is an indispensable base of modern economic growth; that this means, particularly in the older countries, a major dislocation of people settled on the land for centuries; and that one of the crucial problems with respect to currently underdeveloped countries is how such a costly shift—costly in terms of equipment required and of the destruction of established patterns of life for large groups in the population—can be carried through without social and political deformations that may stunt or distort economic growth in the longer run that follows.

THE SHIFT TOWARD URBANIZATION · If the shift in industrial structure implies technological revolutions in both agriculture and industry, with whatever different costs they involve in the older and more settled countries compared with the younger and emptier countries, the corollaries of this shift must also be noted. A whole complex of changes is embraced under the term "urbanization," in which a large proportion of labor and population in nonagricultural pursuits results, for technical reasons, in the concentration of population in densely settled, relatively large aggregates with numerous consequences to the mode of life. The reason is largely the economy of scale in nonagricultural pursuits permitted by a technology that separates the productive process from land area, an economy that produces increasing optimum-scale units as the technical means of transportation, communication, and organization grow more effective. This economy of scale also means that *pari passu* with urbanization there is a marked change in the scale and nature of the managing unit, whether for organizing economic activity or for organizing social activity at large—from the individual firm to the corporation, from private enterprise to public organization—as the complexity of problems and their impact on society as a whole increase. The growth of the large corporation, public utilities, and government means in turn an increase in the weight of those areas in economic life in which free competition in the usual sense of the term must give way to complete or partial monopoly.

All these processes affect the grouping of population by social and economic status and transform the basic patterns of life. As already indicated, there are the effects on the patterns of consumption which go far toward explaining the rise of service industries that has continued relatively unabated through the recent decades. There are also the effects on population-growth patterns, since it is the urbanization of the population, the growth of the wage-earning and salaried groups and the decline in the relative weight of small individual, nonprofessional entrepreneurs, and the emphasis on individual attainment through long and intensive training that play so great a role in the decline in the birth rate.

Above all it is the interplay of the shifts in industrial structure, urbanization, the character of economic and social organization, consumption (and savings) patterns, and population increase which provides the key to an understanding of the process of economic growth. The emphasis is on the indissoluble tie-in among all of these which renders the sustained rise of population and per capita income more than a matter of a few more industrial plants or a few more railroad miles. The transformation of an underdeveloped into a developed country is not merely the mechanical addition of a stock of physical capital; it is a thoroughgoing revolution in the patterns of life and a cardinal change in the relative power and position of various groups in the population. With the old and persistent patterns in the older underdeveloped countries (which include the earlier stages in those now developed) representing equally close interrelations between population movements, industrial structure, the mode of life, the character of economic and social organization, and the like, the growth to higher levels of population and per capita income involves a revolutionary change in many aspects of life and must overcome the resistance of a whole complex of established interests and values.

Trends in Capital Formation

The accumulation of capital is ordinarily viewed as an important factor in economic growth. Indeed, one has only to look at the physical evidence in industrially advanced countries and recognize modern technology's needs for machinery and apparatus to house and channel its driving powers, to admit that without the heavy capital investment in buildings, roads, bridges, railways, power stations, machine tools, and blast furnaces, high levels of total and per capita product are unobtainable. Capital accumulation must, therefore, be examined and, if possible, its bearing upon economic growth specified.

The most effective statistical approach is by means of estimates of capital formation as one component in national product, either net or gross of current consumption of durable capital. The other component, as used here, is the flow of finished products to the individuals and households that constitute the nation's ultimate consumers. True, this concept of capital omits irreproducible natural resources, which may be a major factor affecting the *direction* of a country's economic growth. But every country has some natural resources, and one may argue that the natural-resource potential is a function of the changing stock of technological knowledge, the very same force whose application calls for the accumulation of reproducible capital. The factors that induce formation of reproducible capital adequate as a basis for economic growth are unlikely to be inhibited by an absolute lack of natural resources.[19]

Capital formation as ordinarily measured includes net or gross additions to the stock of construction (including residential and related housing) and of producers' equipment and net additions to nonhousehold inventories within a country. As a component of total national product, it also includes net changes in claims against foreign countries (excess of exports over imports of all goods and net factor receipts). There is some question of the treatment of consumers' durable commodities other than houses—furniture, passenger cars, and so on—and of military construction and equipment. By and large, the figures underlying the summary below omit consumer durables and include military construction and equipment.

For countries for which long-term data are available (largely the more developed countries, excluding the recently established authoritarian nations as well as most underdeveloped countries, for which data are lacking), the statistical evidence may be summarized under three broad heads.[20]

First, the proportion of gross capital formation to gross national

[19] This is an inadequate comment on a major problem. But the brief discussion reflects a judgment that the supply of natural resources is a secondary factor in economic growth, in the sense that growth can be attained despite poverty in resources (as in Japan and some smaller countries); that in the underdeveloped countries even known natural resources are exploited at a much lower rate than in the developed; and that many countries, with a wealth of valuable natural resources, such as Brazil through much of the nineteenth century and Venezuela today, are still underdeveloped. This position does not imply a denial that, once a combination of factors favorable to growth exists, the availability or lack of certain natural resources would affect the *direction* of growth, the distribution of its emphasis among various industrial sectors of the economy; nor that the dependence of modern technology upon certain natural resources creates a drive, on the part of rapidly growing large states, to acquire control over the supply of such resources, with effects on external relations among units to be discussed below; nor that the availability of economically valuable natural resources is a factor, although not of the first rank, in the constellation that affects economic growth, with consequences for the geography of the spread of the industrial system during the nineteenth and twentieth centuries. But in this brief sketch, it seemed justifiable to set this problem aside as less crucial than the others discussed.

[20] See the author's "International Differences in Capital Formation and Financing," in Moses Abramovitz, ed., *Capital Formation and Economic Growth* (Princeton, N.J.: Princeton University Press, 1956).

product ranges from over 10 to over 20 percent; that of net national capital formation to net national product, from about 5 to about 15 percent. The upper limits suggested are particularly firm in the sense that no higher shares are found for periods of two decades or more. Even in Japan, where the proportions have been particularly high within the period covered by available data, these limits have not been exceeded. This means that flow of goods into ultimate consumption has been by far the dominant proportion of current product: not much less than 80 percent of product gross of current consumption of durable capital and more than 85 percent of net national product.

Second, while estimates reaching back into the early phases of industrialization or before are scanty and their margins of error naturally wide, there is a suggestion of a phase in modern economic growth in which capital formation proportions were rising. One could argue with some conviction that they must have risen from preindustrial levels when per capita incomes were low and their rate of growth moderate. Indirect support for this contention lies in the fact that in many presently underdeveloped countries, gross capital formation is less than 20 percent of current gross national product, and net capital formation is well below 10 percent of national income. If the surmise is true, there is an acceleration phase in the rate of growth of the capital stock similar to the acceleration phase in the rate of growth of population, national income, and per capita income. The timing of this upward phase in the rate of growth of reproducible capital, for comparison with the timing of accelerations in the rates of growth of the other magnitudes, would be of particular interest. Unfortunately, the current data and analysis do not permit comparison.

Third, for the countries for which long records are available (and they are the ones with particularly rapid rises in per capita and total income), the increase in capital formation proportions, if observable, ceases well before the recent decades. In some countries even a long record shows no upward trend in these proportions and, in fact, shows a decline in the *net* capital formation share in national income. Thus in the United States, for which we have estimates back to 1870, the ratio of gross capital formation to gross national product has been, on the whole, stable, and that of net capital formation to national income has declined. This difference in trends is due to the increasing share of charges for capital consumption in gross national product, and the latter is due in part to a temporary rise in the ratio of the stock of capital to current product and in part to a shift in the composition of capital away from the longer-lived types (e.g., buildings) toward the shorter-lived (producers' equipment).

These observations have some bearing upon the ratio of the stock of capital to output, a ratio that has recently been widely used in economic analysis. If we deal with net output and with capital net of accumulated depreciation, the relation between the capital-product ratio and the current proportion of net capital formation to national income can be easily seen. If we assume that national income (in constant prices) grows 4 percent per year and that net capital formation is 12 percent of national income, then on the assumption of stable proportions over a long period, the ratio of accumulated capital stock to annual output will be 3 to 1. To put it differently, a persistent capital-output ratio of 3 to 1 and a growth of 4 percent per year in national income imply a net capital formation proportion of 12 percent.

The capital-product ratios for a few countries suggest several findings in addition to those mentioned above.[21]

First, the ratio of net capital stock to annual national income varies from about 3 to 1 to about 7 to 1. But it is not necessarily higher in the countries with high per capita income. In those countries which are among the younger and have grown most rapidly (United States, Canada, Australia) the ratio is about 3 to 1 or slightly higher. In Great Britain and France it was about 6 or 7 to 1 just before World War I; in Germany, 4.6 to 1; in the Netherlands about 5.0 to 1 (in 1939).

Second, the ratio rose in the two or three countries for which long records are available (United States, Great Britain, France). In the United States it rose from 2.8 to 1 in 1879 to almost 3.8 to 1 in 1919; in Great Britain from 4.6 to 1 in 1865 to about 6.2 to 1 in 1895. But the rise ceased well before the recent decades.

Third, since countries with lower per capita income can have higher capital-output ratios than those with higher per capita income, the ratio of even reproducible capital to output in some underdeveloped countries may well be high. Even if a country's total product grows only 0.5 percent per year, a sustained net capital formation proportion of 3 percent of current product would,

---

[21] Underlying data except for the United States are from Clark, *op. cit.*; those for the United States are from Simon Kuznets, ed., *Income and Wealth*, Series II (Cambridge, England, 1952).

in the long run, yield a capital-output ratio of 6 to 1. Paradoxically, the slowly growing, low-income countries may be more capital "intensive" than the more advanced, rapidly developing ones, if we measure intensity by the magnitude of capital supply per unit of final output.

Some intriguing aspects of the evidence just summarized are of bearing upon the role of capital accumulation in economic growth. The first is suggested by the relatively low capital formation proportions even in the most advanced countries: on a gross basis, the upper limit seems to be 20 to 25 percent. It must be remembered that capital formation includes residential and related housing, which may account for three to four tenths of the total, and net changes in inventories, which are hardly a productive tool that embodies the benefits of technical progress. If capital formation is limited to the strictly productive tools that embody modern technology, that is, to industrial plant and equipment, the proportion of annual additions in national product may be no more than 5 to 7 percent; and the capital-product ratio with such capital as the numerator may be little higher than 1.

True, capital formation estimates are subject to a downward bias even in terms of the concept used here. In the early decades of a growing economy, considerable additions to capital stock may be provided by labor within the enterprise (e.g., the clearing of land by farmers) which escape measurement; in later decades, outlays on research and market development are treated as current expenses and do not enter the capital formation totals. A more important source of understatement is the difficulty of allowing for quality changes in passing from outlays in current prices to those in constant prices. Since quality changes are most marked in capital goods embodying the fruit of technical progress, the understatement is particularly important in that category of capital. But with all these qualifications, the proportion of *resources* devoted to increasing the capital stock that forms the material basis of the highly productive economic civilization of advanced countries is still surprisingly low.

Two answers to this puzzle may be suggested. First, technical progress consists not only of inventions and innovations that require heavy capital investments but also of a stream of relatively cheap changes and improvements whose cumulative effect is a drastic reduction in input of resources accompanied by increases in output. The major capital stock of an industrially advanced nation is not its physical equipment; it is the body of knowledge amassed from tested findings of empirical science and the capacity and training of its population to use this knowledge effectively. One can easily envisage a situation in which technological progress permits output to increase at a high rate without *any* additions to the stock of capital goods.

Second, if technological changes permit huge additions to output with only minor additions to reproducible physical capital, it may be that the essential investments are largely in human beings, the active agents in society, not in sticks, stones, and metal. Even if we disregard the essential social inventions and consider only the material flows, the concept of capital used above is probably much too narrow for an analysis of economic growth. If by capital formation we mean the use of any current resources that adds to future output, many categories now treated under flow of goods to ultimate consumers should be included under capital. Certainly significant fractions of outlays on education and training, travel and recreation, improvement of health, and even on living, insofar as they contribute to the greater productivity of the population, are among these categories. Perhaps this new dividing line cannot be drawn with assurance, but it does seem that if capital is what capital does—contributes to increased productivity—much of what is now classified under consumer outlay in advanced economic societies rightfully belongs under capital. With this change in classification, the proportion of capital formation in national income would be much larger than it is now in the developed countries, but *not* in underdeveloped societies. And instead of a difference in net capital formation proportions between 10 percent in advanced and perhaps 3 percent in underdeveloped countries, the true difference may well be between 30 percent or more and 3 percent.

That the stock and formation of physical capital has meaning only within the full context of economic life and that much of high level ultimate consumption functions similarly to capital formation makes it easier to understand other statistical findings. These findings indicate that some countries with a higher per capita income have lower or about the same capital formation proportions as others with lower per capita income; thus from the 1870's to World War I, net capital formation proportions in the United States were not significantly higher than those in Great Britain, although through much of the period the per capita income of the former was significantly above that of the latter. Even more puzzling is the finding that in all countries for which we have long records, capital formation proportions either do not rise at all or cease to rise after a while, although the upward trend in per capita income continues. These results are the direct opposite of those found in all cross-section analyses within a country at any given time: in such comparisons we invariably find that higher incomes per capita are associated with higher savings proportions.

As already indicated, technological change may make it possible to produce much greater volumes of final product with the same or lesser volumes of *all* resource input or may minimize the need for large stocks of physical capital by substituting training and education of human beings and improvement in the whole fabric of social organization for more machines. In that sense, the high consumption proportions in intercountry comparisons, and their maintenance or rise in long-term growth, may be associated with high or rising shares of categories within consumer outlay that are functionally similar to capital formation. High and rising consumption per capita is usually associated with high and rising proportions of outlay devoted to education and training, improvement in health, and all types of goods beyond basic necessities that contribute to the skill, morale, and efficiency of the population. Finally, in addition to these permissive conditions on the technological side that do not compel high capital formation proportions, there are more directly limiting factors on the savings side. On a country-wide scale, capital formation is identical, *ex post facto,* with savings, and limitations of the former proportion may, in the final analysis, be reducible to limitations of the savings proportion, in other words, to the spending habits of individuals who, in the society under discussion, are the main source of country-wide savings. It can be shown that under conditions that stimulate a continuous rise in the level of living, the savings proportions of the masses of income recipients are severely limited if they are calculated rationally to provide for old age and contingencies; and that the contribution to savings of the groups at the top of the income pyramid, the "automatic" savers, is limited by their small numbers and by their share in country-wide income. The savings proportions may be more limited in the younger and rapidly growing societies than in the older societies since the size distribution of income is less unequal in the former. (Compare the United States, Canada, and Australia with Great Britain or France between the 1870's and World War I.) In long-term changes, the savings proportions may be stable or may even decline slightly because the pressure toward higher levels of living keeps pace with growth of total income per capita; because the shift in class structure may be from those with higher saving propensities (farmers and small individual entrepreneurs) to those with lower (urban wage-earners and salaried workers); because a rise in the share of the top income groups is prevented by high mobility, today's captains of industry giving place to different captains of industry tomorrow; and because in recent decades the size distribution of income has definitely changed toward lesser inequality.[22]

The technicalities of the interplay between the factors determining the country-wide savings proportions and the use of these savings in various types of capital formation can hardly be discussed here. But one aspect should be noted because it bears closely upon the relation of capital formation to economic growth. If savings are limited by the responses of human beings, the effectiveness of capital formation permitted by such savings depends at least in part upon the way these savings are channeled into capital investment. One earmark of an advanced economic society is the variety of organizational forms of capital users and the variety of financial institutions which assemble and channel the savings. This is but another aspect of the thesis already urged that the effectiveness of a given stock of resources, embodied in physical capital, in increasing total output is partly a matter of its uses in combination with other resources and partly a matter of availability of such other resources and of the organizational arrangements for bringing them together. The new illustration reveals that the very choice of particular forms of physical capital, of quality rather than quantity of capital formation, depends upon the existence of institutions that can assure the most effective flow of savings so that they will reach those foci in

[22] This is a highly condensed summary of various hypotheses relevant to a complex and still inadequately explored aspect of economic growth of industrially advanced countries. Further discussion is contained in two papers: "Proportion of Capital Formation to National Product," *Proceedings of the American Economic Association* (May 1952), pp. 507–526, and "International Differences in Capital Formation and Financing," *Capital Formation and Economic Growth.*

Furthermore, as Moses Abramovitz has indicated, the point concerning the productivity-raising function of much of modern consumption expenditures implies that they are also substitutes for savings in the narrower sense of the term. Outlays on education and related activities are in a way provision for a future income and reduce the pressure for savings in the form of property claims; and of course they reduce the true level of disposable income and so cut into the amounts available for saving as ordinarily defined.

the productive economy in which additions to capital stock will
yield the greatest contribution to long-term growth. Without such
an organization some part of savings may be stagnant and lead
to no capital formation and hence to no countrywide savings; or
some may be invested in ways that are far from optimal for economic
growth.

In making these comments one does not deny the importance of
physical capital accumulation as a prerequisite of economic growth.
A certain minimum stock is indispensable to the productive operations that form the content of advanced economic performance: one
cannot conjure up railroad services without a roadbed and rolling
stock. But this minimum stock is a *necessary*, not a *sufficient*, condition; with just a roadbed and rolling stock one gets no transportation services, and even with the addition of labor and fuel, there is
a world of difference between efficient and inefficient performance.
Furthermore, beyond this indispensable minimum, physical capital
is not a prerequisite. Far more important than physical capital are
the economic and social characteristics that reside in the capacities
and skills of an economy's population, that determine the efficiency
of the institutions which direct the use of accumulated physical
capital, and that guide the current product into the proper channels
of consumption and capital investment. These factors make the
problem of economic growth so much more difficult than it would
be if the stock of physical capital were the one really strategic
factor in the process. If the latter were the case, given the ability
of the more advanced countries to produce large stocks of capital
equipment, the attainments of economic growth would have been
far more widespread than they are.

Trends in International Flows

Relations among countries, relevant to problems of economic growth,
are reflected in material flows: either peacetime, "normal" flows of
population, goods, and capital funds across the boundaries or wartime flows, implied in cold war or hot conflict. There is also the
spread of knowledge, ideas, tastes, and preconceptions that is in
some ways even more important. These reveal in part the existence
of transnational resources, of which the findings of empirical science
and the stock of social inventions are the most conspicuous examples, and in part the community of human nature, which expresses
itself in the tendency of discrete human societies organized in

sovereign states to imitate, attract, or repel each other.

Our findings, which are largely statistical, relate to material flows. Before considering them, one should note that the volume of peacetime flows, at least, is partly a function of the way the world is divided into separate jurisdictions among which *external* relations can arise. If the world were one unit, there would be no external flows unless connections were established with other planets and their inhabitants (or with migrants to them, founding sovereign communities). By analogy, if there were only two or three sovereign states, the volume and character of these external flows would also be different. Furthermore, the different sizes of these units, the character of their boundaries, and a host of other geographic factors are all significant for both the economic development of the states and for the flows among them.

In its current (early 1950's) population estimates the U.N. distinguishes 85 independent states. For the sake of simplicity, we disregard the numerous dependencies here; their population is only 0.3 billion of total world population of 2.4 billion, and the economic independence of a political dependency is questionable. Four sovereign states—China and India, the two great underdeveloped countries, the USSR, which is just going through its phase of industrialization, and the United States, the economic leader—account for well over half of the 2.1 billion people living in the 85 independent units. At the other extreme, 39 states, each with a population of less than 5 million, account for less than 70 million, and 31 more states, each with a population between 5 and 20 million, account for less than 350 million. Thus by far the great majority of states, 70 out of 85, account for barely over 20 percent of the total population of independent states.

This somewhat bizarre distribution raises the question whether problems and study of economic growth for these small units, the majority of those in the world, are similar to those for the few large states with populations of 100 million or more today (and whose relative position on the population scale was the same a century ago). True, some characteristics of economic growth are universal. But surely the tasks of organization and integration, sharply posed by the disruptive character, at least in the older countries, of some of the processes involved in modern economic growth, are quite different in a huge country like the USSR or India from those in a small country like Norway or Sweden today, or in Uruguay or Venezuela in the future. The minimum or optimum scale of some modern industries is also of relevance. Finally it is clear that the volume of external flows is affected by the distribution among small and large states, for the proportion of foreign trade and often that of capital flows tend to be inversely related to the size of the country, measured by population or total income.

It would require a separate study to establish whether the current state distribution is very different from that of one or two centuries ago, and particularly whether any trend can be discerned in the structure of states. General impressions are not a safe guide, because there have been movements in opposite directions. Within the two centuries under view there were unification and reduction in number in some states, of which Germany and Italy are conspicuous examples. But there were also many separations and breakdowns: emergence into independence of the numerous sovereign states in the Western Hemisphere, Asia, Africa, and Oceania; dissolution of multinational monarchies of the Austro-Hungarian and Turkish types; and a peaceful separation of closely related but distinct national groups, exemplified by Norway and Sweden or Holland and Belgium. The general impression is that the number of sovereign units is increasing, if one disregards such statistical oddities as the princely states in India or the jurisdictions in early nineteenth-century Germany and Italy (some of which, however, did not bar close economic relations and coherence).

Although this suggestion of an increase in the number of sovereign entities is subject to further statistico-geographical tests, the trend over the last two centuries toward intensification of national organization and feelings has become quite evident. Recent historical research has properly emphasized this trend, to the point of concluding that the cult of nationalism has become the secular religion of modern times, a religion that has rapidly spread from its origin in Western Europe to much of the rest of the world. Although the relevance of this trend to economic growth and to international relations is of interest, we can only note here the whole complex of influences on economic growth of strong national governments, through the enlargement of the internal trading area, the promotion of the security of economic activity, and its assistance to groups that constitute the spearhead of economic advance, as well as the reciprocal influence of technological progress and of a rise in economic productivity on the effective powers of central governments. But one may stress that intensification of nationalism is both the result of pressures generated by economic growth and a tool for overcoming them. For if modern economic growth, like any major change in the social order, requires some groups to make sacrifices and some to face risks, if it requires the dissolution of established positions and values in older countries and independent action in younger countries, there will be a natural tendency to strengthen the integrative ties of nationalism, either in the struggle for political independence or in the attempt to persuade the population to accept the sacrifices and dislocation that seem necessary to achieve the goals of economic growth. This does not mean that as a result of some deliberate calculation there has been a conscious plan to intensify national loyalties for the expressed purpose of inducing people to bear the burdens of economic growth. Yet it is hardly an accident that the first carriers of nationalism have also been among the leaders in the economic growth of their nations; the nationalist creed was adopted by the industrial entrepreneurial classes of the European countries and of some colonies in the late eighteenth and through most of the nineteenth century. Nor is it an accident that in recent decades, the strenuous attempts by authoritarian states to foster nationalist feelings by cultivating the myth of an ever vigilant and powerful enemy accompanied the call for sacrifices at home that were considered necessary to the effort to force the pace of economic growth. Finally, given this interrelation between economic growth and the intensification of the cult of supremacy of the nation (sometimes passing over into the ideal of the monolithic state), the consequences for peaceful and, even more, for warlike external relations are obvious.

It is against this background of the increasing political division of the world that the trends in external relations should be considered. For the peacetime flows, satisfactory data exist as far back as the mid-nineteenth century. Although it is difficult to summarize the evidence without oversimplification, the trends are so conspicuous that the danger of being misled is minimized.

MIGRATION · In the movement of men we are concerned exclusively with emigration and immigration. Tourist movements are included under flow of goods; and temporary border crossings by workers are not too important for economic growth, nor can they be measured reliably over long periods. As for international migration for permanent residence, the nineteenth century saw an increasing volume of *voluntary* movement of people to foreign countries that reached its climax in the two decades preceding World War I and grew to magnitudes, both absolute and relative, hardly to be found in any *free* migrations of earlier times. Intercontinental migrations estimated since the late 1840's were at an *annual* level of over a quarter of a million in 1846–1850 and rose to a peak of about 1.5 million per year in 1906–1915.[23] The addition of intracontinental migration would raise the annual volume of international migration in the decade before World War I to close to 2 million. If total migration was about 0.3 million in the 1840's and 2 million in 1906–1915, it grew more rapidly than total world population, which increased from about 1.1 billion in the mid-nineteenth century to about 1.7 billion in the first decade of the twentieth century. Although annual international migration was not much more than 0.1 percent of the total population, the cumulation of migration over a decade raises this to 1 percent and in evaluating such figures we must recognize the importance of free migration to marginal groups in the populations, most of the latter, for various reasons, being firmly attached to their countries of residence.

The character and function of this migration become clear as we examine the countries of origin and destination. The preponderant portion of intercontinental migration, and even of total migration, was from the older countries of Europe to the younger and emptier countries, particularly the United States. The record for this country reveals that while in the short run of business cycles, migration flows may have been more responsive to the pull of better conditions in the United States than to the push of transiently worse conditions at the source, in the longer run the push has been more important. The national origins of the European flow into the United States, in the succession from the British, to the German, to the Scandinavian, and then to the South and Southwestern European reveal the progressive impact of the dislocation in Europe produced by changes in agriculture and by industrialization (the only major interruption in the sequence was due to the collapse of the Irish economy in the famine of 1842). This largely European migration seemed to have served not only to man the economies of North America as well as some of those of Latin America and the European outposts in Oceania and Africa, but also to provide an escape valve during some critical phases in the modern economic growth of several older European countries. By contrast there was

[23] The underlying data are from Walter F. Willcox, *International Migrations* (New York: National Bureau of Economic Research, 1929), Vol. I, and Woytinsky, *op. cit.*

little international migration of the populations of Asia, when considered in relation to their huge size or even absolutely. And when dislocating impacts of the transition phases to the modern economy did reach some of them, as in Japan, legal barriers prevented large scale emigration to areas with higher living standards and greater economic opportunities.

The abrupt reduction and then almost complete cessation of international migration during and after World War I are fairly well known. Willcox's estimates show a drop in the volume of intercontinental migration to 0.8 million for the rather favorable period of 1921–1924. The tightening of restrictions during the depression decade of the 1930's resulted in a net migration loss in the United States. In 1949, to take a recent year, international migration was about three quarters of a million, abnormally high since it included a flow of over 200,000 Jews into Israel. The reduction of international migration to a trickle, and its shift from a relatively free to a highly restricted process after World War I, is but one manifestation of a violent break in the trends of international relations. Similar changes will be found in flows of goods and of capital funds.

COMMODITY FLOWS · In considering the trends in the flow of goods, our attention will be centered on commodities, since data on services (earnings in international activities of merchant marine, insurance companies, financial institutions, and tourists) are scanty. However, foreign commodity trade is by far the dominant component.

Taking a cross-section view for 1938, for example, we find that the ratio of commodity imports or exports to the available relevant country-wide totals (national income plus imports) varies from a low of less than 1 percent for the USSR, to about 5 percent for a large country like the United States, to as much as 30 percent for countries like Norway and New Zealand.[24] The ratio is biased for several reasons: it is too low because the numerator excludes international flows of services; it is too high because the denominator should be *gross* national product (not national income) plus imports; but most important, it is too low because it should be related not to total national product plus imports, but only to that part

[24] Underlying data for income are from U.S. Department of State, *Point Four*, Publication 3719 (January 1950); and for imports and exports are from the League of Nations, *Network of World Trade* (Geneva, 1942).

which can flow across boundaries. Neither the labor of construction workers nor the labor of physicians and others serving the resident population of a country can be exported or imported; and there are other similar goods. The proportion of such goods to total output is sizable, so that a ratio of commodity exports or imports to national product of 20 percent or more is likely to represent a country's close involvement in and dependence upon the network of international trade. It is primarily the smaller countries that are so involved. The correlation between the export-import ratio to national product and the size of the country, measured either by population or by national income, is negative: for 53 countries in 1938 the coefficient of rank correlation is between −0.4 and −0.5.

If it could be calculated, the world-wide ratio of commodity foreign trade to total output would be dominated by the low rates for the few larger countries, and it would therefore be highly untypical in the sense that it would combine these with the high ratios for a multitude of small countries. But it seems likely that through most of the nineteenth century, certainly since the second quarter and up to World War I, the volume of foreign commodity trade (and probably of services also) grew more rapidly than the volume of world output; and therefore an over-all ratio of the volume of foreign trade to unduplicated world output would have shown a significant rise. The quantum of world commodity trade tripled between 1850 and 1880, and then tripled again between 1880 and 1913, thus rising to nine times its original level.[25] During this period, world population increased only about 60 percent, so that the ratio of world commodity trade to population must have risen from 1 to about 5.5. Per capita income rose only in the most advanced countries. On the generous assumption that world per capita income doubled over the period, the ratio of world commodity trade to total output would have almost tripled from 1850 to 1913, and the increase was probably greater than that.

This rise in the ratio of the volume of foreign trade to world output before World War I did not necessarily result from the rise in the ratio in all or even in most countries. The records indicate that in a country already in the network of foreign trade and entering the phase of rapid growth of population and of industri-

[25] Underlying data are from Loreto M. Dominguez, *International Trade, Industrialization and Economic Growth* (Washington, D.C.: Pan American Union, 1953), mimeographed.

alization (with consequent large rises in total and per capita income), the ratio does not necessarily rise. In the United States, for example, it has in fact drifted downward slightly but perceptibly since 1870. The movement of the world-wide ratio was very likely the result of the extension of the orbit of world trade to countries that had not participated previously; and this in turn resulted from improvements in transportation and communication facilities. The *absolute* volume of flows of goods across boundaries increases with a country's economic growth and industrialization, barring the drastic changes in policy involved in an Iron Curtain. But it may well be that in the process of growth, the rising proportion of goods that cannot enter into international flows, and the effects of shifts of activity away from the country's boundaries may offset the effects of improved transportation and communication and result in a downward rather than upward trend in the ratio of international flows of goods to national output.

The implication of the consideration just advanced is that even if there had not been any violent disturbances in international relations, the marked rise in the ratio of world foreign trade to world total output might not have continued, but the retardation in this rise, and the possible decline, would have been gradual over many decades. What in fact happened is that the rate of growth in the absolute volume of foreign trade dropped abruptly beginning with World War I, and the ratio to world population and output must have declined. In 1913, the index of foreign trade was close to 300 (with 1880 as base year), and by 1947–1951 it was close to 400. Thus from 1913 to 1947–1951, a period of three and a half decades, world trade increased about a third, whereas in the three decades before World War I it tripled. Since World War I, world population has grown 40 percent, and world per capita income has also probably grown somewhat. Therefore the ratio of world trade to world production has probably declined significantly since 1913–1914.

CAPITAL MOVEMENTS · External flows of capital funds (foreign capital investments, short- and long-term) are largely a function of the international flows of goods: a country accumulates credits either by exporting more than it imports or by leaving earnings of existing investments abroad. It is, therefore, not surprising to find parallelism in the trends in international capital flows and in the flows of goods. The major difference is in level: capital funds are *net* balances resulting from *gross* flows of goods across boundaries and the relative proportions of the former in national product (or wealth) are much lower than those of the latter.

The ratios of capital imports or exports to domestic capital formation were, in some cases, sizable.[26] In the United Kingdom the share of net capital exports in net domestic capital formation for the period from 1870 to World War I ranged from one third to nine tenths, and in gross domestic capital formation, from one fifth to two thirds. In France, the other major creditor country of the nineteenth and early twentieth centuries, the share of capital exports in domestic net savings ranged from one third to four tenths. In some debtor countries (Sweden, Canada, Denmark) capital imports accounted for substantial shares of domestic capital formation, but this was not true of a large country like the United States nor, as far as the records indicate, of Japan. Since capital formation is a relatively limited share of national product, the proportions of capital flows to the latter are quite low. About the highest ratios shown are 6 to 7 percent for capital exports in the United Kingdom in the decade before World War I, and over 9 percent for capital imports in Canada in 1901–1910. But most shares in national income or gross national product are well below 5 percent.

From 1870 to 1914, international capital flows were at their highest, and international indebtedness in 1914 was the result of capital imports and exports during a period that, historically speaking, was most favorable to international movements. At the end of that period total international debt (short- and long-term, adding only net credits for creditor countries) was somewhat short of $50 billion. Whether this is a large or small amount depends upon the base with which it is compared. In 1912 the value of total reproducible capital of the United States alone was $94 billion, and the rate at which foreign capital was being loaned from 1870 to 1914 was clearly a small fraction of world capital formation, and even less of total output. There were just a few creditor countries—the United Kingdom, France, the Netherlands (to a smaller relative extent), Germany, and a few smaller countries—and their number and economic magnitude were limited vis-à-vis the potential debtor countries. Furthermore, their capital exports were kept down, partly

[26] Underlying data are from the author's "International Differences in Capital Formation and Financing," and from United Nations, *International Capital Movements During the Inter-war Period* (New York, 1949).

by the limitations on their *total* savings and partly by demands for the latter within the country.

A goodly share of the total capital exports was channeled into destinations justified by political rather than economic considerations. Of the total foreign investments of Great Britain, almost half were within the empire; of French foreign investments, close to half were in Russia, Turkey, the Balkan states, Austria-Hungary, and her colonies; and of Germany's investments, about one third went to Austria-Hungary, Turkey, Russia, and the Balkan states. Although in some cases economic and political considerations may have coincided, and in others the line of distinction cannot be drawn sharply, a sizable proportion of foreign capital investments was probably motivated by political considerations. Hence the amount available for countries in which conditions were conducive to economic growth was smaller than the over-all amount.

Before 1914, the trends in the proportional importance of capital exports and imports seem clear. In the two major creditor countries, the United Kingdom and France, the share of capital exports rose to a peak in the two decades just before World War I. In the debtor countries, capital imports tended to become less important as the country grew (Sweden, Canada, the United States, and Australia) and there were definite indications of a coming reversal to creditor position. The upward trends in the outflow proportions from the creditor countries are not inconsistent with the downward trends in the inflow proportions in each debtor country for which a long record is available: the total incomes of the latter were growing at a significantly higher rate than those of the former, and the number of debtor countries was increasing.

World War I had particularly marked effects on three major creditor countries, the United Kingdom, France, and Germany, and the whole network of foreign investments was drastically transformed by rapid drafts upon balances, cancellations, war debts, reparation obligations, and other financial claims. Although it is difficult to summarize post–World War I developments, several aspects seem clear. First, the disturbance of international conditions meant a sharp reduction in the response of capital funds to economic needs. Second, the isolation after World War I of a sizable sector of the world community in the USSR and the shift in the role of the United States to that of main creditor, with its lesser dependence upon and involvement in the network of world commerce and international division of labor, meant radical changes that were adverse to sustained growth of international trade and foreign investments. Third, no matter where the line is drawn between economic and political demands for the flow of funds, the relative importance of political demands has definitely increased since 1914, and the total volume of economic flows of capital across the boundaries has probably failed to keep pace with the growth of world population or output since 1914.

Aggression and Warfare

The abrupt reversal since 1914 of trends in world migration, trade, and capital flows, associated with the international dislocations of which the two world wars were the culminating points, brings to the fore the role of armed conflicts in the economic growth of nations. We have already suggested a relation between the intensification of national organization and feelings, on the one hand, and the pressures and strains of economic growth, on the other, and thus a relation between economic growth and the divisive tendencies that provide a favorable climate for war. But regardless of this and other possible relations, the quantitative importance of such conflicts prevents us from putting them into the pound of *ceteris paribus* or of exogenous factors, and any discussion of economic growth that disregards them is unrealistic. Major wars and their aftermaths have been with us since 1914, and even if we view the period from the Napoleonic Wars to 1914 as an interregnum of peace, and disregard the rather sizable conflicts that punctuated it—the Crimean War, the Franco-Prussian War, our Civil War, the Boer War, and the several Balkan conflicts—a large proportion of the two centuries since 1750 was dominated by wars that affected many members of the advanced economic community of the world. And even in the "peaceful" decades many warlike elements operate in the external relations among nations. Any covert or overt threat of the use of a nation's force in external relations is a form of attack, aggressive or defensive, and armed conflict is only the culmination. Such elements of aggression were widespread throughout the two centuries under review, as evidenced not only by the colonial policies of the major countries but also by sharp breaks and clashes of policies among the European states (and their descendants) themselves. The reversal spoken of above is not so abrupt after all; there were similar strains earlier in the political distortions of capital and of trade flows and in emigration and immigration policies.

It is impossible to summarize here the long-term trends in the use of aggression in international relations; whole libraries have been written on the subject, and it does not lend itself to condensation in the form of statistical totals or unequivocal qualitative statements. Perhaps a summary is not even necessary, since only the broadest outline is needed, and the reader is familiar with the historical record of the major European communities and their offshoots in the New World, in their relations among themselves and with other nations. Instead of attempting a summary I shall consider three questions: What is the association between economic growth and the tendency of a nation to introduce aggressive elements into its relations with the rest of the world? What factors make it likely, if not inevitable, that elements of aggression culminate in wars of major proportions? What are the effects of such wars on the economic growth of the nations engaged in them and of those that are neutral?

AGGRESSION AND GROWTH · Rapid economic growth of a country, once it is of a certain size, seems to be associated with extensive expansion (which often means aggression) or with the exertion of pressure on other reluctant nations to accept changes desirable to it. Great Britain, the rapidly growing economic leader in the late eighteenth and through most of the nineteenth century, thus extended its power and enforced a pax Britannica through much of the world. The United States extended its territory by purchase or by minor wars in the nineteenth century, opened up Japan by the Perry mission, and acquired control over the Philippines. Japan, once opened up, displayed aggressive tendencies through much of its modern history. Germany used wars as stepping stones to further expansion. This association does not mean that aggressive elements exist only in external relations of sizable countries experiencing rapid economic growth; they easily arise out of other conditions. But there do seem to be some almost compulsive factors in a rapidly growing country, provided it is of some minimum size, to display aggressive elements in its external relations with others.

There are cases that seem almost opposite: a retardation in economic and social growth, the decay of once powerful or leading societies, that tends to give rise to aggression because of the power vacuum created. Through much of the nineteenth and early twentieth centuries, the Turkish Empire, the "sick man of Europe," was a chronic source of quarrels, intrigues, and aggressive actions on the part of its would-be heirs among the European powers. And clearly, an indispensable condition for the imperialist policy of economically advanced countries is the "backwardness" of the to-be-dominated societies, their different social structures, which, from the point of view of the aggressive powers, must be modified to favor the proper level of economic intercourse.

In short, large disparities in economic and social conditions among nations that are within reach of each other are often associated with elements of domination by the economically advanced units over the others. Shifts in these disparities, because of rapid growth of new units or because of relatively rapid decay of others, often produce elements of aggression by which the new leaders attempt to claim the perquisites of economic power, or the old and surviving leaders attempt to deal with the new weakness that may have arisen.

A multitude of factors produce the association just indicated, but we are interested primarily in those involved in the process of economic growth. They can be seen most clearly in cases of rapid economic rise. There is first the purely permissive element; aggression means the threat of force, and the latter is largely a matter of the ability to transport power to the area threatened. Rapid economic growth often means rapid increase in this power disposable outside the country, a result both of accumulation of resources within the country and of concurrent changes in means of transportation and communication. But if aggression becomes possible, it does not therefore become necessary; and it is the compelling factors that are crucial. Here we must look for elements of attraction in the use of aggression. The basic one is, of course, that extension of the area over which economic resources of a given country can be used, in proper combination with outside resources, natural or other, is likely to result in a greater per unit product and reduce the risks involved in economic growth.[27] Economic growth is a risky process; for the individual firm it may mean commitments difficult to achieve and for a country it may involve specialization and the need for resources not available within its own boundaries. The leaders of a rapidly growing country may try to minimize such risks by using the power of the state to

[27] See the emphasis on the economic value of sovereignty in R. G. Hawtrey, *Economic Aspects of Sovereignty* (London, 1930). The discussion here uses several of Hawtrey's ideas.

assure access either to raw materials or to markets outside its boundaries.

Two corollaries deserve emphasis. Rapid economic growth usually means a more intensive international division of labor; the leader countries obtain raw materials from areas where natural conditions favor their production and give in exchange industrial products. Such intensification of international trade and capital flows, which is possible only with a higher level of economic performance in leader countries, may require that countries formerly outside the orbit of international trade and investment adopt arrangements that would make more intensive connections with the rest of the world feasible. Nations could "live at home," but only by sacrificing the advantages of close economic intercourse, advantages for both advanced and underdeveloped countries. Since such advantages are greatly enhanced by a given nation's rapid economic growth, we can say that extension into "empty" contiguous territory or the imposition of open-door arrangements upon a "backward" country is a positive function of the economic level. We thus have the natural sequence of attempts to impose rules of economic behavior upon countries that are reluctant to enter the orbit of world foreign trade, from protection of the traders of the advanced countries and the foreign planters of raw materials, to concessions for building railroads to transport the raw materials, to pressures for political changes to assure the safety of the long-term foreign investments represented by railroads, and so on.

Pari passu with this real increase in the advantages of a larger base (either to rule over or to trade with) that is the usual consequence of a country's rapid economic growth, there is the emergence of a "theory" that may easily dominate the views of the country and its leaders. Rapid growth is evidence of success which lends assurance to the country and its leaders that their economic and social practices have proved right, that their views on organizing society for economic functions have met the test of success, and that if adopted in other countries, they would be equally successful. Further, this success persuades them that they have a responsibility to widen the scope of application of this successful type of economic organization, to urge adoption of some of its basic features by those countries that have not been successful and for their eventual benefit. There is a strong feeling of economic and social superiority in the doctrine of the white man's burden and in Point Four activities, as well as an element of the obligation of the successful to the unsuccessful. Such a point of view, if held with sufficient intensity, may easily lead to aggressive action, despite the best of intentions.

All this need not add to a compelling necessity of rapidly growing nations to extend the base of their operations by the threat of force. But the pressures toward such action, combined with the very process of rapid economic growth both in the way of increase of prospective real advantages and the widely held theory of benefits to all from the spread of the successful form of organization, are strong indeed. If in addition such aggression is viewed in the historical context as a correction of past wrong (because non-beneficial) aggressions, that is, as "liberation"; or if it is viewed as preclusive in that if it is not committed by one country, it will be undertaken (presumably in much worse form) by others, the pressures become all the greater. Finally, as already suggested, rapid economic growth may often be the outcome of internal struggles over the problem of industrialization, with intensive nationalist feelings created to help some groups of the population to accept the burdens of economic dislocation. Aggression may seem more justifiable in the spirit of such nationalism and in a sense as a relief from the continuing strains and resentments.

AGGRESSION AND MAJOR CONFLICT · We may now ask why these elements of aggression result in major wars. They need not do so, because the threat itself may produce the desired changes, or even if the conflict actually breaks out, it may be minor in terms of the economic resources that are committed and wasted. A detailed discussion would require a more precise definition of a major war, and it is difficult even to specify what a war is, since conflicts range from a few casual brushes of frontier guards to the protracted deployment of mass armies equipped with all the awesome weapons of advanced military technology.[28] But it is sufficient for our purpose to define a major war as one in which several large countries of relatively advanced economic position are involved over a period of time; the extent of commitment is exemplified by the two recent world wars and by the Napoleonic Wars.

When so defined, the question of major wars can be answered in broad terms. In general, overt conflicts occur when there is disagreement about the relative power positions of the rivals, when the

[28] A valuable compendium on the subject is Quincy Wright, A Study of War (Chicago: University of Chicago Press, 1942).

eventual outcome of the possible struggle is viewed differently by the several camps. For when there is agreement on the result of the use of force and the conviction that force will be used, there is little incentive to engage in war. This is not to deny the possibility that a conflict may be begun by some countries without strong conviction of success, but even these may prove upon closer inspection to have been entered upon in the hope, no matter how slender, that the resultant change in the combinations and alliances of power may bring effective help from major sources previously unengaged.

Indeed, the rationale for many wars lies in just this difficulty of measuring the power potential of the contestants to be devoted to the struggle, and even more in the difficulty of forecasting the effects of the conflict, once initiated, upon the alliance of power in the several camps. Hindsight wisdom is dangerous, but in retrospect it does seem that many wars began with quite opposite views of the contending forces about their true relative power: the Franco-Prussian War, our own Civil War, and the Israeli-Arab War are three examples. Clearly, both contestants could not be right, and one was proved wrong; if true knowledge had existed in advance of the conflict, there might not have been a conflict. Likewise, some hopeless struggles have been entered upon by the weaker camp in the belief that assistance would be forthcoming as the struggle progressed, or at least that the cost of direct surrender would be minimized. Of course in some cases the commitment to a conflict may have been truly irrational, with practically no hope of benefit. But, again, it is the uncertainty that surrounds calculations of relative potential power which breeds warlike policies in an atmosphere of Wagnerian splendor.

If this is the explanation of the development of aggressive elements in external relations into overt conflicts, the preconditions of major wars become clearer. Like all conflicts, major wars will be initiated because of uncertainties about relative strength, measured against the losses in position that may be sustained without conflict; in short, they occur because of errors in judgment on the part of one contesting group. But the conflict cannot be a major one unless several large advanced economic societies are engaged, and unless these units in the opposing camps view the struggle as one in which the costs of defeat are so high that the utmost exertion is warranted to avoid it. The assumptions are that there are several large advanced economic units in the world, that they have available means of transportation and communication by which they can come to grips with each other in armed conflict, and that their scales of social and other values differ enough so that they will be ready to strain their advanced economic power to the utmost.

Against this background, the chronology of major wars during the recent two centuries assumes a semblance of order. The Napoleonic Wars appear as a drawn-out contest in which the protagonists were the two major advanced economies of Europe: France, which was already losing its relative position despite its political revolution, and rapidly growing England. The following interregnum of "peace" appears as a period in which the new rising industrial powers—the United States, Germany, and later Japan—attained a position that challenged British leadership and eventually led to World War I, and later, with the addition of the newly risen power of Russia, to World War II. The rapid growth of the modern economy, of industrial power and technology, the rise and intensification of nationalist feelings, the combination of industrial power with progressively different systems of social values, all contributed to the two protracted and exhausting world wars.

If the economic cost of major wars is largely a function of economic power already attained, the remarkable economic growth of the advanced countries is, *ipso facto*, an explanation of the enormous growth in the economic costs of major conflicts. The permissive relation is obvious; there is much more economic power to waste. But it is the compulsive relation that is more important and perhaps less clearly perceived. Given the intensity of the struggle, human resources are more valuable because of their higher productivity in the advanced countries than more easily reproducible physical capital; and it is possible, within limits, to substitute expensive machinery for the more precious human beings. The greater propensity, in wars between the more and less developed nations, is for the former to have a higher ratio of physical equipment per unit of combatant personnel and a lower human casualty loss. The consequences in the way of high economic costs for advanced countries and wide physical destruction in the less developed countries are also easily observed.

EFFECTS OF WAR ON ECONOMIC GROWTH · The question of the effect of major wars on economic growth is answered to some extent by the comment just made on the enormous rise in costs of major conflicts. Since the positive returns on these costs are at best changes in relative position rather than absolute gains in economic output, the effects upon economic growth are likely to be negative.

A more penetrating view of the problem can perhaps be secured by distinguishing three types of costs involved. First, there is the direct waste of resources, represented by the destruction of human lives and economic goods, varying in absolute and relative magnitude with the extent of participation, the vulnerability to armed attack, and the destructive power of current technology. The tremendous increase in these direct costs, as a function of higher levels of economic technology and of the greater intensity of the overt conflicts, was emphasized in the comments just above. Second, there is the opportunity cost of war, caused by the interruption of the advance of technological knowledge and efficiency in the production of peace-type goods that accompanies diversion of resources to military uses. In wartime, production of some civilian goods ceases altogether and market conditions for the civilian goods still in production do not demand higher levels of efficiency than have already been attained. Third, there is the dislocation cost of wars, their disruption of the international framework of the world economy. The postwar adjustment to the new international situation is neither easy nor quick. The prewar growth of many countries may have been geared to an established and properly functioning network of international economic relations; and because the restoration of this network after a major war is protracted and perhaps never completely successful, depressing effects on growth may be substantial and lasting.

Although measures are not available (except for direct costs), all three types can be illustrated by the experience of the United States in World War I. This country's direct participation in the conflict was relatively short; yet the outlays, both in war casualties and materials and in unrequited assistance to allies, were substantial. The opportunity costs seem to have been even greater. The diversion of resources from the production of consumer and peace-type goods after 1914, well before the country entered the war, led to low construction levels, undermaintenance of the peacetime production apparatus, and an accumulation of gross inefficiency in the economy at large, the consequences of which were felt at least until 1923. Still more sizable in the longer run were the costs of major dislocation in international relations caused by World War I. The whole period from the early 1920's through the Great Depression of the 1930's was probably dominated by the violent disruption of international relations between 1914 and 1923.

Prompt recognition of and adjustment to the changed situation would have dictated different policies from many that were followed. The latter, in retrospect, were sound only in terms of the prewar, more "normal" framework of world economic flows. Because a major war means drastic and rapid breaks in established international relations, many of the costs of the unsound developments in the 1920's and the 1930's must be charged to World War I. To put it differently, if the war had not occurred, there would probably not have been the sharp breaks in international migration, volume of trade, and capital flows; the economic growth of this country would probably not have slowed down as markedly as it did after the first decade of the twentieth century; and there would probably not have been the severe international depression that occurred in the 1930's. The argument that these consequences should be charged to the failure to appraise the changed situation and make the proper postwar adjustments is specious, since this failure was itself a function of the rapid and extensive dislocation that a major war implies.

The offsets sometimes noted in discussions of war impacts, when viewed against these three types of costs, are of uncertain value. It has been argued that a war absorbs otherwise involuntarily unemployed resources of men and machines. This can hardly be significant, since a major war effort requires resources far exceeding any idle reserves and usually is an enormous strain on an economy, even in a country not in the area of combat. It has also been argued that major wars in modern times have accelerated, albeit for purposes of destruction, the application of some basic scientific and technological findings, and thus have reduced the period of gestation of important inventions. But it is difficult to appraise the net contribution of such an acceleration. We do not know what might have happened, nor can we properly evaluate wartime technology in peacetime terms. In the absence of a basis for measurement and because the comparison involves some hypothetical alternatives, the conclusion must necessarily contain a large element of judgment. In the light of the protracted economic difficulties faced by many advanced countries after both major wars and of the deceleration of the rate of growth in this country after World War I and probably also after World War II (certainly compared with pre-World War I rates), the judgment here is that major wars tend to depress economic growth in the participating countries. This means that for a country that has already slowed down in its growth and entered the phase of decline in relative position, participation in a major conflict, on the winning or the losing side, strengthens the trend toward retardation. For a country that is still in the phase of vigorous economic growth, participation in a major war may mean a sharp break in the upward course of its economy.

The opportunity and international dislocation costs are relevant also to the economic growth of nonparticipating countries. Unless these are isolated, a major war brings them a period of high, almost feverish economic prosperity. Combatant countries increase the demand for the neutrals' products and because restrictions on international competition are temporarily lifted, the neutral countries will find additional markets in other countries. But at the same time the supply of important producer and consumer goods ordinarily turned out only by the advanced economies virtually ceases. This combination of abnormal conditions tends to make for a rather distorted and costly economic structure in the nonparticipating countries. The cessation of war and the gradual return of the former combatants to world markets may then produce a reversal in which the neutral countries' economic gains prove to be largely illusory. On net balance the opportunity cost of the war years and the dislocation costs of the postwar period may far outweigh the larger production and greater money returns during the war years proper.[29]

Theoretical Proposals

The summary of empirical findings and related explanatory conjectures presented above is incomplete in that it omits some pos-

[29] I am aware of the inadequate treatment here of the possible positive contributions of war to technological and other advances, and of the bias that may have crept into my judgment of the net balance, but in our present state of knowledge and with the present analytical tools, no fully defensible conclusion can be reached.

However it did seem to me that in much of the discussion, scholarly or popular, the more conspicuous cases of war-induced technological changes, as well as the apparently energizing effects of war effort, tended to blind the observers to the manifold ways in which wars represent losses from the standpoint of peacetime economic growth. In this connection much of the analysis in John U. Nef, *War and Human Progress* (Cambridge: Harvard University Press, 1950) is relevant.

sibly important observations; it is perhaps too venturesome in that it advances speculations without adequate qualification; and it is probably unbalanced in that it devotes too much space to external relations among nations compared with that devoted to long-term changes in their internal structure. But our aim was to survey the similarities and diversities of economic growth during the last two centuries in order to indicate the task of any adequate theory, rather than to offer a complete summary of empirical findings; and to suggest the interrelations and implications that some of the findings convey, not to present completely tested and qualified explanations. If we have discussed at too great length the external relations among nations, particularly the aggressive elements, it is because we feel that they have been unduly neglected—given their importance in past history and the close ties between them and other factors directly involved in the economic growth of nations.

In order to point up the contribution of the preceding discussion toward a theory, we now restate with a possible change of emphasis the lines of approach that are indispensable in any theoretical construction. This can be done best by listing the groups of processes, the strands that seem to be woven always into the fabric of economic growth and seem sufficiently distinct on the surface, even though they are basically interrelated through the factors behind them. At least five such topics, for which there are subtheories, should eventually be united into one theory of economic growth; these are population growth, growth of the stock of knowledge, long-term processes of internal adaptation to growth potentials, external relations of national units, in both cooperation and conflict, and interrelations among all these complexes and the distinguishable components within them. A brief comment on each should indicate the major questions that would be the concern of a possible theory.

POPULATION GROWTH · The task of the theory of population growth seems clearest, perhaps because our stock of organized empirical data is among the richest. To put it simply, we know, in broad outline, the trends that have occurred and the list of relevant factors, but we have little tested knowledge of the relative weights of these factors. Without such weights, we have no theory in the sense of a body of relations to which we can attach coefficients tested for the limits of their variance under diverse conditions in space and time. It is such a theory that must be sought.

The ultimate test of theoretical analysis is in the extrapolative value of its conclusions. Can they be transferred outside the body of empirical observations from which they have been derived and be proved valid under other conditions? In this connection it is relevant to emphasize that purely empirical extrapolation or projection, even in a field like population growth, which we all tended to view as much more stable than the purely economic magnitudes and relations, is a poor substitute for such a theory. A striking revelation of misplaced confidence in empirically observed "stabilities" has been the recent experience with projections of population growth in this country. That these projections, based on extrapolation of our records of birth and death rates for different age and sex groups, proved to be, within a decade or less of their release, so far off the mark is clear evidence that the temporal variability of empirically observed trends is far greater than was generally believed before World War II.[30]

In attempting to develop a theory of population growth, even one limited to natural increase and thus avoiding the complex questions of international migration, we face two major difficulties. First, the decline in death rates, complex as the set of forces producing it is, can occur without an accompanying improvement in economic and social conditions that will assure at least a stable product per capita, let alone a higher one. Death rates in British India declined from about 26 per 1,000 in the 1920's to below 20 per 1,000 in the 1940's; yet there is little evidence of any increase in the low real product per capita. Death rates can apparently be changed by factors exogenous to and relatively independent of economic development; hence this aspect of a theory of population growth must take into account the rather difficult and complex range of possibilities in the realm of medical and public health progress, relatively unbound by the limitations of an economic potential.

The second group of complexities is related to the birth rates. It has in general been assumed that once initiated, their long-term decline, associated with a variety of economic and social transformations, is bound to continue until all groups of society have been affected. The recent upsurge in birth rates in the economically advanced societies is still somewhat of a puzzle with respect to

[30] In this connection see H. F. Dorn, "Pitfalls in Population Forecasts and Projections," *Journal of the American Statistical Association* (September, 1950), and several articles by J. S. Davis published since 1949.

size, duration, and impact. However, it suggests the possibility that in the advanced societies where changes in birth rates play a greater role than changes in death rates in affecting the rates of natural increase, the birth rates have become a more sensitive and variable phenomenon than they were in the past. In other words, in the underdeveloped societies where death rates may be more important in the near future, it is their relative independence of the limits set by economic performance that makes the prospective task of theory so difficult. In the advanced societies where birth rates are more important, it is their recent departures from downward trends and their greater sensitivity to changes in economic and social conditions that constitute an obstacle to the formulation of an adequate theory.

GROWTH IN THE STOCK OF KNOWLEDGE · That the accumulation of empirical and tested knowledge is at the base of the enormous growth of population and economic production during the recent two centuries is a truism. If evidence is required, a glance at the productive structure of any advanced economy will quickly reveal the huge proportion of its activities carried on in industries and by techniques that were completely unknown one or two hundred years ago, and that represent the practical application of much of the basic work in the natural sciences. Indeed, because this relation is so obvious, we referred to it only casually in discussing economic growth as manifested in per capita income, in the shift of industrial structure, and in the division of product between consumption and capital formation.

But no such omission is possible when we consider a theory of economic growth and of the determining factors and their interrelations. For the rate at which additions are made to the stock of tested knowledge will affect the rate at which that knowledge will be applied in economic production, and the latter may spell important differences in the rate as well as structure of economic growth. And this difference, which we cannot measure in our present state of ignorance, between modern times and the earlier centuries in the rate of additions to scientific knowledge must account, in large part, for unusually rapid rates of economic growth in recent centuries. What is true of this comparison over longer spans may easily be true of comparisons within the recent period. We cannot, therefore, take the stock of knowledge for granted; we must learn whatever we can about the causes of additions to and changes in it; we must have some theory of its production and accumulation.

The wide scope of this task must be emphasized for the proper understanding of what is involved. In separating the application of technical knowledge from the stock of useful knowledge, we distinguish between the stock available and stock used and concentrate here on the former. But *all* empirical knowledge, all scientifically tested information, no matter how abstract and remote it may seem, is potentially applicable in economic production. Science, no matter how abstruse, is analysis of the world around us, and economic production is one type of manipulation of this world. This obvious identity of the object of concern explains the chain of connection between the most "useless" cogitations and experiments of scientists often completely unaware of the practical potentialities of their work and revolutionary transformations of the basis of economic production that sometimes flow from them. All empirical knowledge is thus potentially relevant to economic production.

It follows that the very classification of types of relevant empirical knowledge, ranging from historico-geographic specific observations to experimental data, to principles, theories, and generalizations, and to combinations of all of these in inventions, improvements, and practices, is a major task in itself. There are gradations here from the broadest principles to the more specific inventions which may still require protracted testing and pilot plant tryouts before they can be applied on a significant scale in economic practice; from the collections of the most specific data in geology, meteorology, astronomy, and anthropology, to the most general type of abstract tool for operating in the field of theoretical analysis. The institutional conditions under which these bodies of knowledge are produced are vastly different; the patterns of cumulation and "laws" that govern their growth are not likely to be the same in theoretical work on basic principles and in work on accumulation of experimental data, such as boiling and melting points and molecular structure of organic compounds. Yet in the long run, social decisions that affect these conditions may have the most profound effect on economic growth. One need only consider the policy that authoritarian states display toward biology and the social sciences, or the domination of research by the needs of emergency warfare, to recognize that continuation of such practices for a sufficiently long period may have far-reaching consequences for the progress of human knowledge and hence for the potential of growth.[31]

We, therefore, need a theory of the production and accumulation of empirical knowledge, even if for years to come this may mean nothing more than an attempt to learn about the processes involved and the factors that seem important. We already have some hypotheses and reflections; any student who has concerned himself with the economic growth of nations to the point of deriving prognoses or policy conclusions almost inevitably makes assumptions concerning the progress of knowledge and its effects on economic production. It may be better to call explicitly for a theory of production of such knowledge as an indispensable focus for direct and continuous concern with the complex of forces involved here and with their effects on economic growth.

INTERNAL ADAPTATIONS TO GROWTH POTENTIALS · The internal adaptation of a society to growth potentials afforded by the population or by the stock of knowledge has been the chief concern of economic theory in connection with problems of growth. It is in this area that the discipline of economic analysis has made its greatest contribution.

To begin with, the earliest and basic task of economic theory was to demonstrate the interrelation joining individuals and groups in society to the origin and distribution of the social product. The most important function of the economic discipline was to show how a social phenomenon results from individual acts—how market, quantity, and price flow from the behavior of thousands of buyers and sellers in accordance with rules of economic rationality. It is no accident that the main contribution of the Physiocratic School, recognized as the founder of modern economics, takes the form of a *tableau économique*, that the distinctive features of economic analysis are various schemata of "reproduction," demand-and-supply schedules, and similar constructions, which are models intended to show both the connections between units, grouped by their mode

---

[31] To suggest even further complexities of the task urged in the text, one should note that there is not only growth of knowledge, but also revision of it by the continuous substitution for inadequate data and theories of others better geared to rising standards of reliability or to more tenable analyses of expanding bodies of tested observations. Any attempt at measurement of the stock of knowledge must, therefore, be made in cognizance of the continuous changes in standards that shift the qualitative characteristics of existing knowledge. But this is no reason for not urging more emphasis on direct study of the complex of activities and results involved in the accumulation of knowledge.

of action, and the results in the form of either a market or national product, price, and allocation of resources and returns.

This emphasis on the interconnection of the various elements in the total economy of a country (usually classified according to their particular function, e.g., supplies of labor and of other productive factors, consumers, sellers, buyers, and savers) is what makes economic theory so relevant to the analysis of policy problems. It creates an awareness of the effects of any policy decision on *all* groups in society, not merely on some special interests that may be backing it. But it also makes economic theory an indispensable background in the consideration of problems of change, of which economic growth is one. The interconnections among labor, land, and capital in production and the interplay in distribution of units in the market (which is the mechanism by which the interconnections are effected) are basic for a theory of economic growth as long as the economy remains a system of interdependent parts in growth, as it does when viewed for the sake of simplicity in terms of static circuit flows. But in using the concept of the economy as a system of interrelated parts, we must avoid transferring to economic growth the limiting assumptions of static theory.

One way of adapting the articulated analysis of static interaction among the components in an economy to the problem of economic growth is to identify certain carriers of the latter within the system; the addition of capital via savings can thus be viewed as a passive condition and the dynamic function of the entrepreneur (the profit-maker) as the energizing element. Given such an entrepreneurial group, responsible for making the proper choice in the combination of productive factors, given a propensity for savings by which additional resources can be made available to the entrepreneurs, and given the interrelation between supply and demand for capital goods (savings) identical with that for other goods, economic growth can be visualized as a rise in total output within the framework of an interdependent system that moves forward to higher levels.

Entrepreneurs and capital formation are the minimum elements that must be added to the static conception of a circuit flow to make economic growth possible. But there can be marked variations in emphasis, as well as in the extent to which these additional elements in the theoretical system will be permitted to effect continuous changes on the interrelations. There are significant differences among the views of Adam Smith on the growth process as caused by the expansion of the market which results in increased division of labor and the competitive action of entrepreneurs watched over by the state to prevent the collusion to which they are prone; those of Malthus and Ricardo, who shared the conviction that pressure of population growth and exhaustion of land would make the entrepreneurs (profitmakers) helpless against a progressive reduction of their share in the nation's product, and hence against the arrival (considered fairly imminent) of the stationary state; of Karl Marx, whose labor theory of value provides the basis for the theory of exploitation, and who conceived of capitalists as a historical class driven toward greater and greater capital accumulation by the unavoidable decline in the rate of surplus value (the base of their profits) and toward the destruction of competitors and the increase in the proportion of the proletariat in the population, all eventuating in a revolutionary debacle; and of Schumpeter, who views the entrepreneurs as an elite group of innovators capable of overcoming the resistance to change of the traditionalist and numerically preponderant groups in the economy, and are likely to fail in the end only because their very success tends to strengthen the elements of society that inhibit their actions and provide an increasingly unfavorable social climate for their operation.

We indicate these differences—and they are so large as to produce different prognoses and different policy bases—to show that it is not enough to have a hypothesis that explains how economic growth is *possible*, as each of these theories does. It must also demonstrate how such growth *occurs* in the real world, and what factors in what combinations produce the particular adaptations of the economic systems in various countries to the potentials of economic growth. If entrepreneurial action and capital accumulation are to be stressed, the theory must still show how the factors determining these elements produced similar or different results, in the broad terms of a given background of historical experience.

In this connection, it is illuminating that the views just noted can be traced to somewhat different historical backgrounds. Granted that the whole intellectual climate, the basic *Weltanschauung*, of these authors differed from the rationalist background of Adam Smith to the inverted Hegelianism of Marx to the partly "hero in history," partly "elite" ideas of Schumpeter, yet one may argue that the historical canvas of the major technological changes whose application required the innovating type of entrepreneur and the institutions of banking that could finance him, which are given prominence in Schumpeter's theory, did not exist or were in embryo in Adam Smith's time and could hardly have played an important part in his analysis. Similarly, Smith could not have observed the disruptive effects of the Industrial Revolution in England, which colored so much of Marx's and Engels' study; nor could these effects loom as large to the twentieth-century economists, who are more concerned with the current problems of their day. Likewise we have noted the effect of the isolation of England during the Napoleonic Wars as well as the growth and mobility of its population upon the original and rigid (and it is the one that persisted) formulation of population and diminishing returns theory in the Classical economics of Malthus, West, and Ricardo. Such tracing of general theories to their historical background can only be suggestive at best. But it does seem that important differences in emphasis on the interrelation between the dynamic entrepreneur and his environment in producing economic growth reflect different phases of the growth experience itself. As long as economic theory is largely a response to current problems, it is likely to be affected by the immediate historical background. It follows that the construction of an adequate theory of internal adaptation of an economy to the potentialities of growth must be made with cognizance of the danger of concentrating on too limited a segment of history and must face the challenge of dealing with an adequate variety of growth experience. Such a theory must, in particular, reach beyond establishing the *possibility* of economic growth to formulate the important factors, with due effort to bring some testable order into the sequence and variety of phases that an internal adaptation of an economy to the potentialities of growth may display.

This leads to the question of parts of the economy and society other than those selected as the dynamic carriers of change or the providers of additional tools for them. Some of the comments made in the summary of empirical findings indicate that these elements are important in a theory of internal adaptation of a country, for it is in their gradual (or sometimes rapid) modification that the key to possible growth may lie. The theories noted above contain some references, explicit or implicit, to these other sectors in the economy. The Malthus-Ricardo analysis of longer-term trends in the distribution of national product points to the expected changes in the position of labor and in the share of landlords. The Marxian prognosis specifies the proletarianization of the masses of society, their increasing misery, and so on. One could go through the theories also in search of statements or inferences concerning the role of the state and find again significant differences ranging from its role in Classical economic theory in the way of enforcing competition and rationalizing the system of justice, education, welfare, and services, to the Marxian concept of the state as a tool in the hands of the capitalist classes, to some of Schumpeter's suggestions concerning the role of the state as a possible carrier of some survivals of precapitalist times and the organ through which the growth of elements inimical to the innovating entrepreneur may find expression. Such observations on the trends in the role of the "passive" elements are indispensable.

The reasons for specific emphasis upon this segment of the theory of internal adaptation is that here may lie the greatest contrast between the explanation of how economic growth is possible and the explanation of how it is actually realized. Given the dynamic elements, the carriers of change, we can demonstrate how economic growth is possible. To demonstrate how it is realized, we need in addition the interplay of these elements with all the other major groups and forces in the economy. Indeed, closer examination and more thoroughgoing study of the interrelations in the process of economic growth may show that the distinction between active and passive elements is false in its very sharpness. The literature on the entrepreneur as the focus of economic change suggests too much tautology; all change is enacted by human beings, and if we identify those that make changes as entrepreneurs (or profitmakers) without at the same time specifying the group apart from their actions, we explain economic change by definition rather than by substantive analysis. Yet a study of the origin and performance of entrepreneurs—defined substantively as all decision-makers, not tautologically as carriers of change—might reveal that the conditions that produce them and determine their effectiveness are intertwined with the conditions and factors that govern the behavior and the capacity for change of all other groups and institutions in society. Of particular relevance here are our earlier comments on the role of the state in making decisions to relieve the strains produced by economic growth, and on the role of physical capital and savings proper in relation to the consumption patterns and attitudes of the masses of consumers and workers. If this interconnection among all components in the process of economic growth persists, it is indispensable to incorporate in the theoretical analysis all the factors, passive and active, that determine the pace and structure of

growth, factors that may be reflected in the changing functions of
the state, the trends in character and composition of the labor
force, the evolution of financial and other institutions, and the
long-term changes in business structure. In concentrating on the
presumably strategic elements, for instance the entrepreneur, we
risk neglecting the other elements, particularly since some of them
are believed by many economists to be outside the proper concern of the economic discipline.

If the theory of internal adaptation must weigh fully the factors
involved both in the dynamic elements that provide the primary motive power and in the willing or unwilling response of all other important groups and institutions in society, and in the process test the validity of the distinction, the most feasible approach may be by explicit
and comprehensive attention to the sequence of structural changes
accompanying economic growth. The discussion of empirical findings conveys an impression of relative persistence and uniformity
in the character of such changes, be they "industrialization," "urbanization," increase in scale of operation, greater degree of impersonal organization, or those changes connected with the distinction
between consumption and reproducible capital formation. Some
structural changes not specifically discussed (e.g., changes in the
size distribution of income) may also reveal significant association
with economic growth defined as the sustained increase in per capita
product. Furthermore, because at least some of these shifts reflect
either persistent traits of human wants or a common complex of
technological knowledge, they may be found in economic growth
under different forms of social organization, in the authoritarian
states as well as in the libertarian democracies.

In any theoretical analysis, such a close association between the
rate of economic growth and the changes in structure may become
an important explanatory link. If per capita product grows, and if
simultaneously certain structural shifts occur, the latter may explain
the next stage of economic growth and some of its corollaries, both
internal and external to the national unit. A *stage* theory of invariable sequences need not necessarily be attempted. But if such
sequences recur often, the empirical data accumulated can perhaps
be best organized with the help of a theory that uses changes in
structure to set up phases in modern economic growth and attempts
to formulate and test both active and passive factors and their
interrelations against the background of what might be called
typical *reference* phases of economic growth during the recent

epoch, or, even more ambitiously, of similar phases distinguishable in several epochs of economic growth.

EXTERNAL RELATIONS OF NATIONAL UNITS · The theory of external relations is an extension of the theory of internal adaptation. If the latter can establish the ties among various factors that determine economic growth within a country, the analysis should presumably have some validity for the flows among nations. The industrial and other changes accompanying economic growth within a country usually mean shifts in relative rates of growth of the several regions and changes in location of industry. Thus any theory which, in accounting for the internal adaptation of a country to the potentialities of economic growth, explains shifts from agriculture to industry and the mechanism of the flows of labor, goods, and capital by which this is accomplished should also shed light on the flows of labor, goods, and capital among nations at different phases of their development.

This observation seems particularly valid for the theoretical analysis of peaceful types of external flows, with international migration analogous to internal migration, the flow of commodities and services across boundaries analogous to such flows among regions or industries within a country, and flows of capital funds in foreign investment analogous to domestic flows of capital investment. Indeed, much of the contribution of economic theory to the understanding of problems of world trade and capital investment lies in its service in explaining the basic features of economic processes within a country and then in applying these explanations, with such simple but concrete modifications as the assumption of relative immobility of labor and the emphasis on diversity of natural resources among the nations, to international flows.

A similar observation has bearing even upon a theory of aggressive external relations. For if the analysis of internal adaptation assigns, as, it must, some role to the state, its performance within the country will suggest some inferences concerning external relations. If the major function of the state is to provide security and justice within the nation, as a basis for the beneficial effects of free competition and division of labor (under compulsion, if necessary), its role on the international scene is likely to be to protect the nation and strive for international division of labor, even if the latter entails an element of aggression. If the state is viewed as a repressive mechanism, a tool in the hands of the dominant classes, it is likely to be viewed as such outside the country's boundaries. It is significant that Classical economics, which interprets the state as a benevolent watchman and assistant at home, presents a relatively peaceful picture of external relations, whereas the Marxian School, which views the state as a tool in the hands of capitalist classes within the country, stresses imperialist aggression and exploitation.

Conceived as an extension of the theory of internal adaptation, the analysis of external relations naturally becomes an analysis of the spread, peaceful or violent, of the patterns of economic organization and growth from the more to the less advanced countries. If the same factors drive a given country forward to its more advanced stages and determine its relations with other countries, they are also likely to act on the "other" as they did on the less advanced sectors within the given economy. Thus Classical economic theory implies the inevitable spread of industrialization and economic growth across the world, radiating via international trade and capital movements from the leading national units, and the Marxian theory implies the spread of exploitive imperialism with the absorption of precapitalistic countries into the network of world capitalism.

Limitations of the theory of internal adaptation will therefore be reflected in limitations of the theory of external relations. One should note in this connection the underemphasis on the roles of various political and social institutions in the process of economic growth within the country, a natural consequence of the tendency of economists to concentrate on their own discipline and to carry these "noneconomic" variables as qualifying exceptions or as "special" doctrines not incorporated into the body of theory (note the treatment of noncompeting groups, the general view on the nationalistic doctrine of the protective tariff, and the like). Paralleling this underemphasis is a conspicuous neglect in the field of international relations. Thus, the assumption of internal mobility of labor or capital in response to purely economic differentials, which, however qualified by references to social, racial, and other barriers, does not incorporate them into the corpus of analysis, is likely to be paralleled by a similar difficulty in dealing with the much wider legal, cultural, and other obstacles in the international flow of labor and capital. Incorporation of these obstacles, if they are sufficiently important, may lead to an assumption of complete immobility rather than one of unrestricted mobility. But neither oversimplified model provides the basis for fruitful theoretical analysis. There are obvious analogies too between the underemphasis and overemphasis of aggressive elements in the role of the state within the economy and in external relations.

Earlier comments concerning the general direction of further work on the theory of internal adaptation—a more explicit consideration of the roles of all major economic and social institutions, and particularly of the state, and an attempt to distinguish their interrelations against the background of some recognized framework of phases in the recent epoch of economic growth—bear with equal force upon the theory of external relations. There is no need to repeat them here. We only add that neither theory will be complete without the other. Given the technological possibility of material (and hence of spiritual) flows among nations, the internal adaptation of any country, advanced or backward, cannot be explained without some understanding of its relations with the rest of the world. The sequence of structural stages in the process of growth and any associated changes in the level and time patterns of the rate of increase in total or per capita product must involve the competitive and cooperative relations in the spread of an economic epoch from one nation to the next. The internal adaptation of a country to the potentialities of the modern economic epoch, whether we call it "industrial capitalism" or, more properly, the "industrial system," is at the same time an adjustment to its existence or absence in other parts of the world. By the same token, external relations can be understood only as an extension of the processes of internal adaptation, modified by the cleavages that are greater among than within nations.

INTERRELATIONS · That the four distinct aspects of economic growth and the various components within them are interrelated need hardly be mentioned. This interrelation has been stressed in discussing internal adaptation and external relations; it certainly applies to population growth, which is related to accumulation of knowledge and to the structural changes that constitute the essence of internal adaptation which in turn affects external relations; and it is implied in treatment of the economy of any given country, or of a large part of the world, as a system of interrelated parts, in growth as well as in static-flow analysis. Even in the case of accumulation of knowledge, perhaps the freest variable among those outlined, economic and social institutions may determine, if not the direction and rate of progress in basic scientific theory, at least the chain of processes by which basic scientific discoveries are translated into a stock of tested knowledge which in turn becomes the basis for inventions and applications. Indeed, since empirical knowledge can be fully tested only by ramified application, and since such application is part and parcel of economic and other activity of large groups in society, the production of the stock of tested knowledge can hardly escape being linked in the whole chain of interconnections and reciprocal determination that binds together population growth, economic development, and the structural changes within the country and in the framework of international relations.

Hence, a discussion of the theory of interrelations as a separate topic in the outline of a prospective theory of economic growth is artificial and unnecessary. It is artificial because it would hardly be possible to treat one of the four topics without continuously referring to the others, which at some junctures appear as determinants and at others as effects. It is unnecessary because one could hardly add anything to the suggestions bearing upon such interconnections already made in the discussion of empirical findings, unless the scope of the empirical findings were broadened or our probing were made more intensive by means of additional data. We can only state more explicitly the questions we must face in trying to synthesize into a unified theory of economic growth the wide range of processes and factors hinted at above. These questions bear upon the possibility of formulating a unified theory for nations of different sizes, nations at different stages of the spread of a specific type of economic system, and nations with distinct characteristics of social and political organizations. This possibility leads immediately to problems involved in distinguishing one major epoch or type of economic system from another, and the question whether a unified theory of economic growth can apply to more than one epoch in the long history of society.

Whether one should devise variants of a theory of economic growth for the many small nations different from those for the few large ones is a question that has already been raised. It may well be that analysis would indicate that growth in the smaller countries, particularly in the more advanced ones, depends upon close economic ties with some large country, and that the changing fortunes of the latter determine the growth of its smaller satellites. It is granted that no nation, however large, is completely independent and also that the smaller units may remain relatively more independent, as long as they also remain underdeveloped. Further analysis may show, however, that the advance of the small nations is contingent upon their becoming members of a larger economic constellation and that for them the recent methods of relative isolation and forced industrialization under self-contained, authoritarian auspices are not conducive to economic growth. Without prejudging the answer, one may stress that at the point of synthesizing the different strands in the analysis of economic growth, the problem raised by the contrast in size in the present (and past) distribution of national units must be posed explicitly.

There is a difference in patterns of growth between the nation that is the pioneer in a new economic epoch and those that follow, just as there are differences among followers in the sequence of their entrance. In our modern epoch, the simple listing of England, the United States, Germany, Japan, and Russia suggests marked differences in the pattern of growth as these countries entered the phase of industrialization, and there seems to be significant association between at least some of these differences and the fact that each entered the industrialization phase with a different number of predecessors already in the field.

The possibility of variants in the theory of economic growth is suggested by the different questions that one tends to ask in dealing with a pioneer country and its followers: for the former, why *it* was the pioneer; for the latter, what obstacles had to be overcome in following the example. Another relevant observation, already made, is that the very increase in the number of large units that have attained fairly high levels of economic growth is likely to have taken place under, and in turn produced, conditions favorable to increased incidence of major wars.

The question posed by differences in social and political structure is closely associated with the sequence in the spread of an economic system from one major country to the next. If a new phase in economic history emerges, its appearance in the pioneer country will occur in a specific historical setting, a given social and economic structure, and will produce some important changes in it, as the agricultural and industrial revolutions did in England. The follower countries have a different historical heritage; it is this difference that makes them followers rather than pioneers. Hence, as the new system spreads it will affect countries that are significantly different in their social and economic structure from the pioneer at the time it entered the new era. Furthermore, the time lag between the pioneer and the followers will be some function of the difference between the political, social, and cultural heritages: the wider the difference, the longer the time lag. In addition, the latecomers will be adjusting to the potentialities of the new system under historical conditions quite different from those of the pioneer or even of the early followers.

It is, therefore, likely that the changes that accompany the shift will also be radically different. The late entrance of Japan and Russia is to some extent associated with the differences between their historical heritage and that which produced the early entrance of England and the United States, and the different political and social structures that evolved in them are a result partly of the differences in historical heritage, partly of differences in the world scene. In oversimplified terms, the authoritarian character of late industrialization may be rationalized as the response of a backward country that is not concerned with new inventions and discoveries since a rich stock is ready for adoption by imitation; that has as its most plentiful resource human labor, unskilled and unaccustomed to the individualistic cooperation which results from a long investment in education, political democracy, and the like; and that uses human labor to pay for the primary capital accumulation necessary for industrialization. Whatever the explanation, a question arises concerning the variants in the theory of economic growth needed to treat adequately the variety of political and social characteristics that may accompany the growth process, as a given system spreads to national units with historical heritages different from those of the pioneers and early followers.

The consideration of differences in political and social structure and their effect on economic processes leads directly to the definition of an economic epoch, of a type of economic system. Thus, if we shape our theory to account for growth of nations within the system of "industrial capitalism," it is to be questioned whether the USSR is a unit of the species and whether our theory should account for its growth experience. If we deal with the "industrial system," by which we mean an economic organization that applies extensively the results of modern science to the problems of economic production, but not necessarily under private business auspices, the USSR definitely belongs to the category and the theory must account for its growth experience. This question whether or not the projected theory should cover the growth of nations under industrial capitalism or under the industrial system or, for that matter, should also encompass such earlier epochs as merchant capitalism, the agrarian empires of the East, and the medieval town economy—is surely a major one and influences both the organization of empirical findings and the eventual attempt at synthesis of the various sections in the theoretical analysis.

The empirical evidence summarized here has been limited to the last two centuries and, largely for lack of data. to countries that operated under the auspices of libertarian democracy and the business system. As suggested above, there is good reason for limiting the organization of evidence and the formulation of a theory of economic growth to the experience of the last two centuries. One common thread in the empirical findings reinforces this decision: the rates of growth of both population and per capita income were exceptionally high; the shifts in the internal structure of the economies that have led in economic growth were rapid and widespread; the impact upon the country and the reactions of political and social institutions within the country and in international relations were far-reaching and violent; the diversity in growth experience among various countries was marked and the resulting differences in economic levels were striking. Even allowing for the myopia that may afflict the contemporary or near-contemporary observer, there is ground for viewing the last two centuries as a distinctly new epoch, an epoch that in the acceleration of the rates of economic and social change seems exceptional. As a matter of intellectual strategy, we might limit the immediate task to a theory of growth of nations under the industrial system (this does not preclude supplementation by similar attempts to distinguish the persistent relations and sequences in earlier epochs since much of the recent past cannot be clearly understood without them). But in this limited period of the last two centuries, the theoretical frame of reference should not be confined to countries that experienced economic growth under the business system. It is more useful to take the view that the authoritarian latecomers also are adapting themselves to the potentialities of technological and social invention for greater command over economic goods or economic weapons.

Ultimate Uses of the Theory

This bare outline of a theory of economic growth of nations under the industrial system of the last two centuries covers an extremely wide area, transcends the usual limits of the discipline of economics, and may seem so demanding as to be impracticable and useless. In a sense, nothing is easier than to prepare overambitious blueprints, and few intellectual exercises may be as futile. Likewise, given the division of labor among disciplines, it is easy to chide economics for neglecting related social phenomena which, however important in economic growth, may be viewed by economists as beyond their professional competence. Furthermore, criticism of faults of omission may be gratuitous if the omission is compelled by a structure of the discipline that has advantages for the treatment of other problems. These dangers were always lurking in the background during the writing of the preceding section. But they were offset by the hope that the goals set would encourage rather than inhibit the search for relevant empirical evidence and for more adequately formulated and closely knit theoretical analysis. In discussing the limitations of past economic analysis in the field, there was no intent to deny that these theoretical constructs rendered an immensely useful service in dealing with other, chiefly short-term problems, or that they suggested approaches to the analysis of economic growth proper, particularly to growth questions that were in the forefront of attention at that historical conjuncture.

It may help, if not to avoid, at least to limit misunderstanding and disagreement if we conclude with some brief observations concerning the crossing of the limits of the discipline of economics, the attainability of the theory to which the discussion has been directed, and the practical significance of the related work.

RELATED FIELDS · The major observation on the extension of analysis to areas beyond economic discipline proper—to population movements, accumulation of knowledge, political structure, and the like —is that in fact economic analysis does make assumptions, often explicit, concerning trends and relations in these fields. This is a matter of necessity, if the analyst wishes to infer something determinate either about the causes of economic growth in the past or about the prognosis for the future.

A most conspicuous illustration is the treatment of technological change in Classical and Marxian economics. Both systems contain a generalization to the effect that technical progress cannot be counted upon to overcome effects of diminishing (relative to growing population) supplies of irreproducible natural resources, particularly land. In Classical economics it is explicit in the law of diminishing returns from land, formulated as a *historical* or empirical generalization. In the Marxian doctrine, it is implicit in the law of diminution of the rate of surplus value, which is based in turn on the assumption that the reduction in time necessary to produce workers' subsistence *will* lag behind the effects of rise in the organic structure of capital. The plausibility of that assumption is linked to the role of land as a limiting resource in the production of food and other major sources of a worker's subsistence. The stagnation theory of the 1930's assigned a similar key role to technological change. Its proponents claimed that the demand for private capital arising out of new inventions and changes *not* associated with extensive expansion of population and area would fall short of the flow of savings *ex ante*. If such substantive statements about technological changes are a prerequisite for determinate statements about economic growth, surely it is better to recognize this area and the related area of accumulation of knowledge as deserving of major and explicit concern and study, empirical and analytical, than to continue to make assumptions based on general and untested impressions, no matter how obvious they may seem.

The argument applies, indeed, beyond the field of economic growth, to the validity of results of analysis in application to even short-term changes. It is hardly an exaggeration to say that economic analysis faces a difficult choice: either it must admit that none of its results has validity until they are supplemented by findings of other disciplines on the processes impounded in *ceteris paribus;* or it must state where, in real life, *ceteris paribus* begins and ends. The former alternative is hardly palatable; the latter involves an uncomfortably speculative decision. If this view is at all valid, much of the contribution of economic analysis of short-term problems must perforce completely disregard the long-term concomitants and consequences. Whatever the case in the treatment of short-term changes and problems, in the analysis of long-term trends, of economic growth, little in the way of testable results can be expected without explicit treatment of all the areas noted above. Much as one may regret leaving the shelters of an accustomed discipline, it does seem as if an economic theory of economic growth is an impossibility if by "economic" we mean staying within the limits set by the tools of economic discipline proper, even within the broader limits of Classical and Marxian economics and all the more within the much narrower limits that have prevailed since the middle of the last century.

THEORETICAL OUTLOOK · But what is the hope of attaining a comprehensive theory of economic growth which has to be built upon the contributions of so many disciplines in the social sciences and humanities and even in the natural sciences, some of which, like the history of science and technology, are in their embryonic stages? Can one work effectively toward so distant a goal? This question must be faced since the desired theory is not limited to some seemingly axiomatic general principles for policy guidance, or to mathematical and quasi-mathematical models demonstrating by a simple combination of a few variables how economic growth is possible. The theory implies a constant search for empirically identifiable variables and their relations, tested under as great a diversity of conditions as the evidence, available and securable, can reveal.

Two major reasons for working toward this goal come to mind. First such a theory provides an effective framework for classifying and organizing a vast number of relevant findings already accumulated on observed trends and their relationships in time and space. It is illuminating, and suggestive of directions for further research, to see the major lines of economic growth in a variety of countries and the relations between the sustained movements in their populations, total and per capita products, industrial structures, characters of business organization, the role and magnitude of the state, and international flows. In an attempt to pinpoint the major focus of such a theory in further organization of data and analysis, we could begin with the statement that economic growth is a combination of transnational, international, and intranational elements; that among the former the stock of knowledge of mankind and its persistent characteristic as *Homo sapiens* are major; that economic growth within a nation during any historical period is the result of an interplay between the institutions and patterns of behavior it inherits from the past and the strains and tensions created by the potential implied in the stock of knowledge, whether or not this potential is already being utilized by another nation; that economic growth is a costly process, both in the breakage it produces in the inherited complex of institutions and interests and in the opportunity cost of resources it requires; and that because economic growth is so costly (and although resolving the tension created by the opportunities inevitably gives birth to other strains and conflicts) the role of the state and other social institutions is of strategic importance. This statement, which is a capsule repetition of much of the discussion, does provide a base, a cogent and integrated view of a vast field of empirical findings and their relations. It should, therefore, serve as a stimulus toward a more explicit analysis of a variety of data until now kept apart and examined largely by specialists in the various disciplines. In short, if a theory of economic growth is to be not just a mechanical assembly of unrelated parts but is to imply some closely woven relations among the parts, it seems to offer an effective goal in that the acceptance of a central focus in a wide field forces attention to all its parts, stimulates the organization of an increasing body of empirical evidence, and inhibits the easy retreat to oversimplified schemes within the confines of a single discipline.

The second argument is related to this one. We do not need clear assurance that an acceptable theory, useful for predictive purposes, would result. Such a theory calls for variables that are empirically identifiable and testable and that also move in a relatively invariable pattern over time, despite major variations in conditions. It may well be that these variables cannot be found. We may never be able to attain specific measures of the distinguishable factors involved and may be forced to treat the various complexes as indissoluble *Gestalts,* constructs in which the very configurations of the identifiable elements are so important that no weights can be assigned to the elements themselves. But it should be sufficient if the theory at any given stage of its development, from the bare and vague sketch of its embryo beginning to the much richer and more articulated structure of later phases, permits the user to orient himself properly among the variety of data reflecting the diversity of experience, to see the relations, even though of limited persistence, among the various strands in the process, and to evaluate the successive notions or theories which are continuously elicited by changing historical circumstances and which, because they are designed to produce hard and clear answers to current problems, almost inevitably claim greater validity than they possess. The value of the theory lies not in its promise to yield precise predictions eventually but in its capacity to bring an ever-growing body of empirical data into analytical relationships which bind together various processes, and thus provide a continuous revision and extension of our notions concerning the important factors that determine economic growth.

PRACTICAL CONTRIBUTIONS · This leads directly to the practical value of the work guided by the broad theory suggested, whose specific outlines are subject to constant revision. Economic growth, and for that matter other aspects of economic life, are affected greatly by secular decisions made by society, decisions of the type already mentioned, concerning, for example, land, labor, capital, and their disposition within the given society or in relation with other societies. In such decisions, the conflict of group interests, the experience of other countries, and a variety of other forces all play their parts. But the very process by which such decisions are reached involves some theory of economic growth. Thus a particular group tries to pave the way toward acceptance of its policy recommendation by relating it to the long-term prospects of the society at large, by claiming that this specific decision (i.e., for disposition of the public domain in one way rather than another), will yield greater benefits to society as a whole, even though it may also be of particular value to the special claimant group. This type of argument, whether advanced by one of the articulate groups usually found in an overt democracy, or by a dictator who despite his powers finds it necessary to justify his decisions proclaimed from on high, contains a theory of economic growth, the latter defined as the most desirable sustained course of long-term changes for the country.

Frequently these notions are a simplified version of some theory propounded earlier by the professional economist or the professional student of social affairs. This is only natural since the "professional" theory is often an articulate, sophisticated answer to some current problems, developed within the intellectual framework of the basic concepts of economic theory. It is not necessarily based on a variety of empirical findings since such variety would almost inevitably make the task of generalization and of unequivocal formulation of policy impossibly difficult. It is this extremely valuable function that much economic writing and theorizing performs: the formulation of an articulate and broad view of a problem, geared to the current conditions and oversimplified to the point of yielding a determinate answer. Unfortunately, such theories, whether in the corpus of economic doctrine or in the simpler form of widespread beliefs, tend to persist far beyond the time of their relevance, and because of the overgeneralization inherent in them, they tend to claim validity far beyond the limits that would be revealed by an empirical test. Yet these views and notions have practical effects, since they may serve as the basis for important social decisions that have far-reaching consequences. To cite one example, the notion of the relation between international free trade and economic growth certainly facilitated the policy that nineteenth-century England pursued with respect to China. It led to the expectation that the opening of the ports would almost automatically draw the millions of Chinese inhabitants into the framework of international trade and thereby eventually introduce in China the higher levels of economic performance associated with modern economic life. It would be easy to repeat examples of widespread notions that are reflections of theories justified in their original historical setting for a relatively narrow area of application, but indefensible in application to other areas or other times.

If this is the case, the practical value of an ambitiously conceived and almost by definition never complete theory of the type indicated, lies in its double function. One would be to provide richer materials for the successive needs of what might be called policy theorizing, defined as theoretical attempts to produce relatively complete systems that can yield determinate policy answers. The distinction between empirical and policy theorizing is not meant to be invidious; the former is never quite complete, whereas the latter must always be definitive, if only by dint of heroic assumptions. But the distinction does seem useful, since in its absence an impossible burden is placed both on the empirically minded theorist who is blamed for not completing his structure and on the policy-minded theorist who is blamed for making his oversimplifying assumptions and not taking sufficient account of the empirical data. If the distinction is accepted, a most important practical contribution of the theory suggested is that it will provide policy analysis with data and findings more relevant to policy concern than has heretofore been the case. It may also lead to less than universal claims for validity for the policy-oriented notions or hypotheses. It may eventually bring about realization by the general public that decisions must be made on the basis of incomplete evidence and that economists and other experts should not be asked to give hard and fast answers to social problems.

The second valuable function of work toward a comprehensive, empirical theory is in its contribution to the destruction or qualification of the more ambitious (in their claims) theories. Cultural lag has become a familiar concept and need not be elaborated upon. Much of this cultural lag consists in reliance on notions that have been retained too long as "general laws." Granted, the resistance of popularly held ideas to rapid change is an important positive element in the continuity of social life and in the transmission of accumulated knowledge from one generation to the next. But the persistence of many of these notions is the result of the difficulty with which new data and findings of empirical social research can be obtained and woven into more than just a new detail. Insofar as this difficulty is reduced by work aimed at a comprehensive theory of the type outlined above, the latter should have great practical value as a solvent of obsolete notions and as a distiller of whatever validity remains in them.

The immediate relevance here of the free pursuit and communication of knowledge is obvious enough. For if any of the older theories concerning economic growth or social life in general are congealed into a doctrine and given the official blessing of immutability and perennial validity; if they become the basis, no matter how violated in practice, of a policy gospel that is above criticism; and if means of communication are barred to anyone who dares to review the doctrines in the light of new evidence, the consequences can easily be foreseen. The wider view of the theory of economic growth advocated here forces recognition of the mutability of many partial doctrines that claim allegiance because they glorify, consciously or unconsciously, their conclusions. For this reason, an indispensable prerequisite for work toward such a theory is the fullest freedom in pursuit of testable findings, in continuous reformulation of interrelations in the light of additional evidence, and in the spread of accumulated results to ever-wider circles. In turn, this work might serve to reduce the obstacles stemming from the dogmatism that attaches to theories which claim eternal and universal validity.

Reflections on
the Economic Growth
of Modern Nations

THE FOLLOWING pages deal with some wide aspects of economic growth, which must be treated rather summarily—indeed, largely as speculations. Although reference to specific research findings will be made at several points, the major purpose here is to raise broad questions whose implications may illuminate the field of economic growth from new angles and suggest new interpretation and new directions for research.[1]

[1] Some of the empirical material and related analytical hypotheses is included in this volume in "Toward a Theory of Economic Growth," pp. 1–81, and in *Economic Growth and Structure* (New York, 1965), "Regional Economic Trends and Levels of Living," pp. 142–175; and "Economic Growth and Income Inequality," pp. 257–287. Other relevant papers are: "Population, Income, and Capital" in Leon H. Dupriez, ed., *Economic Progress* (Louvain, 1955), pp. 27–46; "International Differences in Capital Formation and Financing" in Moses Abramovitz, ed., *Capital Formation and Economic Growth* (Princeton, N.J.: Princeton University Press for the National Bureau of Economic Research, 1956), pp. 19–106; "Underdeveloped Countries and the Pre-industrial Phase of Advanced Countries" in United Nations, *Proceedings of the World Population Conference, 1954* (New York, 1955), Vol. V, pp. 947–968; and "Quantitative Aspects of the Economic Growth of Nations," a series of papers, the first two of which have been published in *Economic Development and Cultural Change*, V, 1 (October 1956), and as a supplement to V, 4 (July 1957).

A translation of "Sur la Croissance Économique des Nations Modernes," published in Économie Appliquée, X, 2–3 (April–September 1957), pp. 211–259.

Since these speculations reflect an empirically delimited record of economic growth, the limits are indicated so that the reader can judge their relevance. The empirical background is constituted by the economic growth of nations during the last two hundred years—from the mid-eighteenth to the mid-twentieth century. Our records of world-wide economic growth during this period are far from complete, and my knowledge of them is even more limited. The reflections therefore rest upon a partial and, in many ways, woefully incomplete record of a short stretch of historical experience. Yet the growth process so observed is sufficiently varied to raise broad questions which may provide an effective base for reorganizing the observations—for that period and perhaps for some other stretches of historical experience.

The reflections fall under three broad heads: the transnational potential of economic growth; the national exploitation of the growth potential which constitutes the process of economic growth of a nation; and international cooperation and conflict in the process of economic growth.

The Transnational Potential of Economic Growth

We measure the economic growth of nations by the rate of sustained, long-term rise in total product, or still better, in product per capita. One outstanding characteristic of economic growth during the last two centuries, when measured in this rough fashion, has been the high rate of increase in population, total product, and product per capita, at least for what we call the developed countries. Western, Central, and Northern Europe, North America, and selected countries elsewhere—the Soviet Union, Japan, Australia, the Union of South Africa, and in recent decades some countries in Latin America—have all witnessed a rise in population and in economic product per capita which in percentage terms was far greater than in the preceding centuries. This exceptionally high rate of secular rise can be easily documented. An average rate of rise of 15 percent per decade in population and per capita income for long periods was not unusual. Yet this rate means that population and per capita product doubled in less than 50 years and more than quadrupled in a century, and total product doubled in less than 25 years.

This sustained growth of population and product was made possible by the increasing stock of tested knowledge. Knowledge of means of preserving life effected a reduction in death rates, knowledge of natural processes and conditions permitted an increase in economic production, knowledge of social institutions and devices yielded new forms of economic organization, and these were all indispensable for the secular upsurge in population and national product, that is, for the high rate of economic growth. In this accumulation of knowledge modern science played a strategic role. Indeed, one might define modern economic growth as the spread of a system of production, in the widest sense of the term, based upon the increased application of science, that is, an organized system of tested knowledge. If any proof of this proposition is needed, a glance at the products of economically developed nations will suffice: from tractors, chemical fertilizers, and hybridization in modern agriculture, to the steel, steam, and electricity framework of modern industry, to the internal combustion and other engines of modern transportation, the overwhelming proportion of modern production employs tools, materials, and processes that rest upon principles discovered by modern science relatively recently. The current developments in atomic energy and its potential uses are further proof, but there is no point in stressing the obvious.

However, some broader implications have not been sufficiently emphasized, if we can judge by the tenacity of some notions that seem to be inconsistent with them. We attempt to summarize and point up these implications under several general heads.

1. There is a direct connection between the most abstract and "useless" analyses at the theoretical level of scientific work and the most "practical" consequences which take the form of inventions and improvements that spread through and transform economic life. Numerous illustrations can be provided: from Hertz's discovery of shortwaves believed by him to be of little practical value to modern electronic devices and industries; from Darwin's experiments on responses of plant growth to light to modern weed-killers; from Pasteur's work on the crystal structure of chemical compounds to microbiology and its contribution to longevity; and from Einstein's theory of relativity to nuclear reactors.

The reason for this connection is fairly simple. All science is controlled observation of the world around us, and even such disciplines as logic and mathematics provide the mental tools for handling empirical observations. Economic production is manipulation of part of observable reality for the special purpose of providing commodities and services desired by human beings. It is

therefore inevitable that anything that can be learned in a controlled and testable fashion about the observable world can and
probably will become a tool for some desirable modification in the
processes of economic production, that is, the processes of purpose-
ful tampering with the world in which we live.

An important corollary follows. If we wish to take stock of all
the tested knowledge that is potentially useful in economic production, which in fact constitutes one dimension of the transnational
potential of economic growth now being discussed, the view must
be wide indeed. We must include the variety of known technological
practices of proven value, the millions of inventions and patents
that have not yet been introduced, the uncounted items of important
factual information (boiling and melting points; atomic and valence
structures of chemical compounds; maps of the heavens, oceans,
and land), and above all the vast and abstruse theoretical structures
in all the sciences that deal with the many aspects of the natural,
let alone the social, world. The abstract theory or "idle" experiment
of today may in fifty years be the basis of an imposing industry
and the source of a major shift in the productive structure of at
least the advanced economies. No such inventory is possible with
the tools generally available, and much of the difficulty in gauging
the changing role of this knowledge potential of economic growth
lies in the failure to learn enough about this potential.

2. In view of this remark, it seems illogical to discuss the rate
of increase in the stock of knowledge within the historical period
under review. Yet some trends are defined so sharply and seem so
important that it would be foolhardy not to consider them at least
as tentative hypotheses.

A first hypothesis is that the rate of addition to the stock of
knowledge, at least that which bears most directly upon economic
productivity, has been higher in the last century than in the
previous one. Certainly the emergence by the second half of the
nineteenth century of such new scientific disciplines as chemistry,
biology, geology, and microbiology provided a firm theoretical
foundation in economically important fields, where improvements
had previously been achieved almost entirely by trial and error.
Furthermore, there is a marked contrast in the relation of technological discoveries to actual changes between the period of the
Industrial Revolution in England and, say, the twentieth century.
The revolutions in cotton textiles and in pig iron and bar iron
production, and the introduction of steam in the second half

of the eighteenth century were in response to long-felt needs, followed a long search, and were based in at least one case—the introduction of coke in the smelting of iron ore—upon trial and error, with little knowledge of the underlying chemical processes. Here then necessity was the mother of invention, and the period of gestation was long. In contrast, many economically important inventions of the late nineteenth and the twentieth centuries were the results of attempts to apply new scientific discoveries, attempts by people like Edison and Marconi who were not scientists but who understood the scientific advances and were impelled to look for practical applications. Here, the addition to the stock of knowledge came first, and one might say that invention fostered need.

The above remarks may be an oversimplification, but while the hypothesis cannot be fully demonstrated, it does seem plausible and can be explained. To begin with, the stock of knowledge never diminishes: it may be revised because better tools and more cogent theories necessitate modification of some findings, but even this is an addition. Constant accumulation of improved information, accompanied by constant improvement in scientific tools, is likely in and of itself to accelerate the pace of new additions to knowledge. The universe is wide, the variety of its aspects is enormous, and the amount to be learned is great. And it is always easier to learn more from a wide base of existing knowledge than from a base of relative ignorance in which it is difficult to perceive the relation between the "new" and the known.

The point can be restated in terms of the relations among the scientific disciplines. The emergence of modern chemistry redounded to the benefit not only of the "applied" disciplines like medicine, but even of physics, a scientific discipline that had emerged before chemistry. Since they are studying different aspects of one world, the several disciplines are closely related. So long as there are major gaps in the system, even the progress of the older disciplines is often delayed until their sister disciplines are sufficiently mature. This is true even of general theory; and when "practical" application is considered, the availability of knowledge of physics, chemistry, and biology on relatively high levels, makes applications easier.

One important corollary follows. Assume that the rate of additions to the stock of useful knowledge has accelerated, that it was distinctly higher in 1850–1950 than in 1750–1850, or even that the rate was higher in 1900–1950 than in 1850–1900. Has the *utilization* of this increasing stock of knowledge, that is, of the potential of economic growth, kept pace with the additions to the stock? There is always a lag in the translation of existing knowledge into economic and social practices, particularly if knowledge is at different distances, as it were, from wide-scale application. But has this lag, measured as a proportion of the total stock of knowledge not yet utilized, been increasing apace?

The problem has many tenuous aspects largely because it is difficult to gauge the stock of useful knowledge. Since this vagueness affects the denominator and it is not easy to define large-scale application, the ratio, the rate of utilization of the existing stock of knowledge, cannot be estimated; and discussion of its trends is a matter of impressions. Still, if there has been a shift from necessity as the mother of invention, to invention as the mother of new needs and impulses, it is reasonable to assume that the backlog of un-utilized knowledge has become proportionately greater.

This conclusion, if true, would have some major economic consequences. For it suggests that *all* countries have become increasingly "underdeveloped," in the sense that none is fully exploiting the growth potential available to it. It suggests that the economically advanced nations have the advantage of a large growth potential and that the *economic* rationale does not always favor capital exports to the underdeveloped areas. If the demand for capital is represented by a curve in which the vertical axis is the yield of the application of the yet unused knowledge and the horizontal axis is the cost in terms of material investment, entrepreneurship, and the elimination of social resistance, it may well be that in the advanced countries the availability of a large growth potential at low social costs means *domestic* capital demand that leaves little for capital exports. The traditional theory, which argues an economic case for the flow of capital from the more to the less developed countries, may thus be negated, partly because it disregards the possibility of this large growth potential even for the most advanced countries and partly because it minimizes the *social* obstacles to foreign capital investment in underdeveloped areas.

3. If the unused potential of economic growth has increased proportionately, another hypothesis can be assumed: as far as potential technological change is concerned, there is no proximate limit to economic growth.

That a social process, like the economic growth of a nation, has no finite limit would seem, on the face of it, an absurdity. Obviously no society can grow infinitely large. But our hypothesis makes no such claim. We do not argue that the population of a nation can increase indefinitely; it may well reach some nearly stable limit because the birth rate may decline to so low a level as to produce a slight rate of natural increase. Or other factors, such as preference for more leisure or low long-term elasticity of demand for economic goods, may permit and warrant only minor increases in per capita product once it has reached certain high levels. Or international relations may be characterized by conflicts which necessitate the expenditure of increasingly larger proportions of national resources on items that are not part of final product. None of these factors which may set a finite limit to the economic growth of a nation is denied by the hypothesis. But it emphasizes the point that the growth potential that follows from progress in science and technology has no upper limit.

Two distinct reasons can be advanced in support of this hypothesis. First, additions to knowledge are largely the product of the free inquiring mind. If there is no effective restriction—either prohibition or complete lack of support—on the curiosity-motivated explorations of the mind, the search for new theories, new data, and new applications will continue. In other words, since the search is continuously self-propelled and aimed at no fixed goal, there is no *internal* source of a limit. This assumption of the *free* mind is both a qualification of the hypothesis and a partial explanation of the impressive development of tested knowledge during the last two centuries.

Given this continuous play of the free mind, the second reason for an unlimited economic growth potential becomes relevant. And that reason is simply the vastness of the observable universe; or, which is the same thing, the quantitative insignificance of mankind in that universe. The stock of tested knowledge therefore concerns a much wider realm than has yet been exploited by mankind, and theoretically the *application* of knowledge can tap an area that extends far beyond our planet. Not only has the exploitation of our oceans barely begun, not only are many new land areas likely to be more productive because of recent discoveries of new sources of energy, but in these days of interplanetary travel discussions we cannot dismiss the possibility of extending processes of economic production beyond the confines of the earth. Under such circumstances, it is difficult to set an effective limit to the potential growth contribution of the increasing stock of knowledge in the foreseeable future.

This argument, which smacks of science-fiction, would perhaps be unnecessary if the contrary notion were not still being stressed in economic theorizing. The writings of the Classical School emphasize the proximate limits on growth imposed by the diminishing fertility of the soil. Those of the Marxian School imply the same assumption in their analysis of the long-term trends in the rate of surplus value. The reasoning in both instances rests upon the assumed inability of scientific progress to cope with the exhaustion of natural resources. Much of the recent Malthusian discussion argues from the premise of a *natural*, rather than social, limitation upon the capacity of mankind to sustain itself. Granted that an imbalance between population and natural resources at a given (usually backward) level of technology poses major problems, one wonders how, in the light of the advance in science and technology during the last two centuries, the premise of a technological limit upon productive capacity in the long run can be retained.

One may add parenthetically that judgments of "experts" on these matters are likely to be at fault. Experts are usually specialists skilled in, and hence bound to, traditional views; and they are, because of their knowledge of one field, likely to be cautious and unduly conservative. Hertz, a great physicist, denied the practical importance of shortwaves, and others at the end of the nineteenth century reached the conclusion that little more could be done on the structure of matter. Malthus, Ricardo, and Marx, great economists, made incorrect prognoses of technological changes at the very time that the scientific bases for these changes were evolving. On the other hand, imaginative tyros like Jules Verne and H. G. Wells seemed to sense the potentialities of technological change. It is well to take cognizance of this consistently conservative bias of experts in evaluating the hypothesis of an unlimited effective increase in the stock of knowledge and in the corresponding potential of economic growth.

4. The preceding discussion does not touch upon two major problems. The first relates to the factors that determine the rate of addition to the stock of useful knowledge. Granted that no fixed limit can be set to the economic growth potential provided by it, we would obviously want to know which conditions favor a high rate and which do not.

This raises a number of complex questions to which I cannot offer clear answers and on which there is not much organized evidence. Presumably conditions would be different for distinct types of scientific discovery, invention, and improvement. And any systematic consideration of the problem would require some classification of types of knowledge, with distinctions drawn eventually, if not in the first instance, upon some hypotheses concerning the differences in the determining conditions involved.

Consider, as an illustration, research in natural science theory and the kind of question that it raises. The political and social organization of Tsarist Russia did not bar the emergence of a Lobatschevsky, a Mendeleyev, or a Metschnikov. Would the Stalinist regime have allowed enough free play of the mind and hence discovery in, say, the field of biology? Why under the free conditions of the United States was relatively little original work done in the natural sciences at the theoretical level, and so much in the applied disciplines and practical invention? What are the *optimal* conditions for the "production" of basic scientific discoveries? How much valid argument can be distilled from the many propositions advanced recently in the controversy between the advocates of socially directed group efforts in scientific work (Joseph Needham, J. B. S. Haldane, and others) and the defenders of the untrammeled, unfettered, individual scientists?

These questions are illustrative and may not even be the proper ones. They have been posed merely to suggest the problem. Yet, although they may not help to formulate it properly, they do illustrate its long-term bearing. Clearly any developments in the system of values which society imposes upon its individual members, in the conditions under which the men and women who are the living carriers of intellectual progress operate, may, through their effect on the whole climate of opinion, influence the rate at which additions are made to the stock of knowledge. The problem becomes all the more complicated when one realizes that the scientific and technological efforts are not the only important ones. The insights of artists often foreshadow the configurations that touch off the work of scientists and inventors. The Renaissance in Italy, in freeing the eye of the artist in painting and sculpture, was the prelude to the scientific study of man and the universe. The imaginative rather than scientific intuition of Malthus touched off Darwin's theory of evolution. And the incisive insights of the masters of modern art may well pave the way to some scientific movements. To that extent the values and conditions that affect the whole realm of the human spirit and its operation are important.

This may seem like a far cry from the economic growth of nations; yet it is here that the major steps are taken that provide the basis for modern technology and economics. In my own ignorance of this field, I can only indicate the relation and the gap in our discussion.

5. The other major lacuna in our discussion can perhaps be suggested effectively by considering the meaning of transnational in reference to the potential of economic growth provided by the stock of knowledge.

This term is used because the knowledge is presumably accessible to all mankind. There is no national physics, chemistry, or biology, and there should be no national economics or sociology. The law of gravitation and the periodic table of elements hold for all nations, and the laws of economics and sociology, although limited to specific types of social organization and technology, should hold for all societies that reach the relevant state and level of development. Theoretically, knowledge embodied in overt and objective terms is accessible to anyone, regardless of nation, race, or habitat, who has the necessary vocabulary and has acquired the necessary intellectual tools.

Is this transnational quality true also of applied knowledge, the necessary link between generally formulated tenets of scientific theory and large-scale economic production? Granted that the laws of chemistry and even those for the production of pig iron or steel are world-wide, the discovery of the use of coke for smelting iron ore was directly beneficial only to those nations that had good coking coal and adequate supplies of iron ore. One may argue that this discovery originated in England partly because a technological-economic problem peculiar to England in the eighteenth century had to be solved. Neither Holland, which did not have the raw materials, nor Sweden, which had both wood and iron ore in relative abundance, was under pressure to make such a discovery.

Insofar as there is a strong element of need in the process of adding to applied knowledge, there may well be national *biases* in the stock of useful knowledge. The weight of new inventions and improvements will probably be concentrated in those types that seem most useful to the few advanced societies with the greater supply of intellectual resources. In other words, over and above the core of the general transnational type of knowledge, there may be others of vast direct practical importance that are of more value to some nations than to others.

We are here approaching the variety of factors which explain the underutilization of the economic growth potential contained in the stock of knowledge. Most of these reside in the social and economic structure of nations and will be discussed in the next section. But while dealing with the stock of knowledge, we should note the possible skewness in its supply. This immediately suggests limits on the growth potential not noted so far, limits that can be found in the past concentration of work on many of the applications —inventions, improvements, and the like—in certain areas. Such concentration has been due to the uneven spread of economic and social progress throughout the world: those nations that advanced first were also among the first able to spare a greater proportion of human resources for work on promotion of knowledge, a good part of which was naturally directed to their own technological problems. There is of course an element of generality, some transfer value, even in the most specific discovery or invention; but when technological effort is concentrated on specific problems, a substantial proportion of the addition to the stock of knowledge must be more directly useful to some nations than to others. To cite an obvious example: modern technology in agriculture is far more advanced in economizing labor than in economizing land, yet for many underdeveloped countries a technique by which the dependence of agriculture on land could be reduced would be far more valuable.

This implies that at least for certain categories of our stock of useful knowledge, the growth potential is limited by the supply of human effort applied to them. It also suggests that one major requirement for underdeveloped countries is the skilled human resources that would be directed to the task of adapting and adjusting the existing stock of knowledge to the particular conditions and problems of these countries. This kind of adaptation and adjustment is only one of several involved in exploiting the potential of economic growth provided by the transnational stock of knowledge. We can now turn to a more direct consideration of the full range of this process.

Internal Conditions of Economic Growth

It is clear from the preceding discussion that no nation, even the most advanced, has fully utilized the transnational growth potential.

The reasons must obviously be in the lack of some essential prerequisites. We can perhaps secure a preliminary view of these prerequisites by noting the social and economic changes in those countries with the largest economic growth. If we find some general corollaries of economic growth, regardless of country and regardless of political and social conditions, we can reasonably argue that these are indispensable concomitants and prerequisites. And this assumption would be even more plausible if we could detect some direct connection between these concomitants and the satisfactory utilization of growth potentials. Having established these concomitants, we should then be in a position at least to surmise why these prerequisites were lacking in so many areas of the world and resulted in economic backwardness, and why in no country the growth potential can be fully utilized. Here we are concerned only with *internal* conditions and the account will be complete only after we have considered the international relations.

Among the concomitants of modern economic growth are new patterns of population growth, industrialization, urbanization, new patterns of use of national product, an increase in the nonpersonal forms of economic organization, and a rise in the relative importance of economic achic.ement in the scale of social values. This list, manifestly incomplete, can serve as the focus in our discussion, and although the discussion must be sketchy, a broad view of the process may be secured.

NEW PATTERNS OF POPULATION GROWTH · Modern economic growth has been accompanied by a substantial decline in death rates followed by a decline in birth rates, and resulting in a long-term rise in the rate of natural increase. The impact of the decline in death rates was unequal; it was absolutely greater in the young, particularly the infant, age groups; and it was greater in the cities, thus removing the excess of urban over rural mortality rates typical of premodern times. The decline in death rates was accompanied by a significant decline in morbidity rates, and the lesser incidence of epidemics and other health catastrophes, which thus made for a temporal stability in the rate of population growth that was previously unknown. The decline in birth rates, when it came, also had unequal impact: associated with voluntary control of family size, it affected the upper economic and social groups first and then spread downward. Finally, during much of the recent period there was a large volume of voluntary migration—a process by which population in some parts of the world could be and was distributed in better adjustment to economic opportunities.

This statement describes the demographic trends which, with different initial dates in different areas of the world, could be observed between the second half of the eighteenth and the mid-twentieth centuries. The trends are well known, but some of their implications for economic growth need to be stressed. The decline in infant and child mortality which, in and of itself, was bound to lower birth rates, eliminated enormous waste. Under premodern, preindustrial conditions, many children were born and raised but never reached productive ages, and the time and resources devoted to the bearing and rearing of these children were a tremendous economic loss. The reduction in the excessively high death rates associated in older times with population density—in cities, armies, or jails—was indispensable since modern economic growth rests upon concentration of population, in plants, cities, or elsewhere. The increasing resistance to epidemics and other mortality catastrophes and the attainment of a temporally *stable* population growth must have had a marked influence by extending the time horizon of individuals, by freeing them from uncertainty, and by encouraging the long-range planning that is characteristic of modern economic activity. The secular decline in birth rates is in a sense a corollary of the movement in death rates and of the changed view of the power of the individual to control his life span and the number of his descendants.

The indispensability of this modern demographic-growth pattern as a base for modern economic growth must be stressed, because the shift to lower death rates and higher rates of natural increase makes for temporary difficulties during the transition process, which often lead to doubts as to its desirability. Yet clearly this modern population-growth pattern cannot be avoided. As will be argued below, a high valuation of material achievement is essential to modern economic growth. Reducing sickness and death is surely the first goal in material attainment, and minimizing health catastrophes is another. If the population must share this view in order to participate effectively in economic growth, how can it be compelled to delay the measures that increase longevity? How, without shifting to a modern pattern of population growth, can the change be made from the joint, large family, with its patriarchal or matriarchal and nepotic tendencies that stifle individual initiative, to the small, individualistic family that is the appropriate unit for modern societies? Without these changes in social valuation and in family organization, the modern economy cannot operate effectively. It is important to emphasize that this shift in the population-growth pattern and in family structure occurred not only in developed countries of Western civilization, which grew under the aegis of business enterprise, but also in Japan and in the USSR, where antecedent historical and recent political conditions were far different. The limitations on material welfare imposed in these countries assumed, and had to assume, a form and rationale different from those involved in a refusal to adopt the contributions of science and technology to the reduction of the death rate and the contributions of the modern way of life to the reduction of the birth rate.

INDUSTRIALIZATION · The long-term increase in product per capita has generally been accompanied by a decline in the proportion of agriculture and related primary industries. This shift in favor of the nonagricultural sectors, or industrialization, is evident in shares in the labor force, capital stock, and national product. Furthermore, there have been shifts among the nonagricultural activities. In many countries, but not in all, the share of manufacturing and construction, including or excluding mining, has become stabilized after a while; but the share of the service industries—transportation and communication, trade, finance, professional and personal services, and governments—has continued to rise. (To deal here with the many other trends, particularly in the relative income per worker in these sectors, would take us too far afield.)

These trends in the industrial structure of national product, capital, and the labor force can be associated with technological necessities, on both the production or supply and consumption or demand sides. The decline in the share of agriculture in the labor force was due to the combination of a marked secular rise in labor productivity in agriculture, indispensable if part of the labor force was to be released for other uses, with the low long-term elasticity of demand for agricultural products—a reflection of the structure of human wants. On the other hand, the marked secular rise in the share of the service industries was due partly to a rather small rise in at least the measurable productivity of labor in several branches of service but perhaps more to the great secular increase in demand. This increase in turn was due partly to the structure of wants of ultimate consumers, in which the proportion of income spent on health, education, recreation, and the like increases with a secular rise in income per capita; partly to the changed conditions of life, noted below under urbanization, which increased the need for services; and partly to the demands of the developing productive organization of commodity output for more transportation, communication, trade, finance, and, not least, government services.

We stress these technological necessities to indicate the indispensability of the shifts in industrial structure in the process of economic growth. For example, if in order to increase per worker productivity in automobile production larger-scale plants were needed, the concentration of production combined with the dispersion of sources of raw materials and of ultimate buyers would mean more transportation, communication, trade, and finance, and hence a greater share of these service industries in the labor force and national product. If, as will be indicated below, industrialization meant urbanization and the growth of cities required more municipal government, the share of government in product and in the labor force also had to rise. In other words, given the structure of human wants and the technological requirements of greater productivity, the shifts in industrial structure are part and parcel of economic growth. This is so even for a single country, since there are secular limits to the concentration of a country's production on a few branches with reliance on the outside world for the rest, particularly at high levels of per capita product.

The secular change in industrial structure involves shifts in the relative weights and positions of various economic, occupational, and other groups within society. A decline in the share of agriculture in the labor force means a decline in the relative weight of farmers and farm workers in society and the movement of a substantial proportion of their descendants into other pursuits. And this process is usually accompanied by differential trends in income per worker in the several industrial sectors, which means that some groups gain, on a per capita basis, relatively to others. Furthermore, the high rate of rise in per capita product that characterized modern economic growth was accompanied by relatively rapid shifts in industrial structure: in only a hundred years the share of agriculture in the labor force in the United States dropped from over 70 percent to less than 20 percent. Obviously, one of the major requirements of economic growth is the capacity of society to undergo these rapid internal shifts, to make feasible this continuous mobility and redistribution of the labor force and population among the various sectors of the country's economy.

URBANIZATION · By urbanization we mean an increase in the proportion of a country's population living in communities above a specific size, the term community implying a concentration of people within a small area. Whether we draw the line between city and countryside at 2,000, 8,000, or higher, urbanization has been a concomitant of economic growth during the past two centuries.

Urbanization is largely a product of industrialization, although the former may occur without the latter and the latter does not fully account for the former. Theoretically, industrialization is possible without urbanization. An authority, determined to prevent urbanization regardless of costs, could prohibit agglomeration of plants and firms within a small area, could require construction of housing for the workers of a single large plant that would assure low density per square mile, to mention only two techniques. However, the costs would be prohibitive. If the technological criteria set the optimum scale of a plant at several thousand workers, forcing them to live far apart would be expensive in transportation to work, in the supply of services to them and their families, and in the cost of land that could be used for more productive purposes. Similarly, locating related plants at a distance from each other just to prevent urbanization would also multiply costs. The fact is that contiguity of related economic units whenever permitted by the productive process (not in agriculture and other extractive industries depending upon extension of the area) is economical, and the cost of dispensing with it is high. In this sense, urbanization is the economic product of industrialization.

But urbanization goes beyond the necessities dictated by optimum scale and location of commodity-producing plants, in the development of highly specialized functions that are feasible only in large cities. And as the economy grows, the need for these functions will itself generate metropolitan areas as centers of activities like wholesale trade, finance, education, legal services, and government. Whereas these functions are in a sense further aspects of industrialization, they are beyond the mere shift from agricultural and related activities and deserve explicit mention. Their location in proximity to other sources of urban concentration—manufacturing, retail trade, etc.—makes urbanization a necessary corollary of economic growth. It is interesting to note that the considered attempt to avoid urbanization while attaining industrialization in the economic planning of the USSR was signally unsuccessful. Although it may have been a wishful slogan rather than a vigorous program, the fact is that urbanization could not be avoided even in this almost completely planned industrialization process.

But the more important point is the effect of urbanization on other trends and concomitants. It sets the conditions for the decline in the birth rate and the shift toward the small family; it requires a vast amount of internal migration, since the cities, particularly in the early days, grew largely by influx from the countryside and this migration meant detachment from roots and easier adaptation to changing economic opportunities; it throws people together so that they can imitate and learn from each other much faster; it facilitates the development of the impersonal relations of modern life, and at the same time teaches cooperation on this impersonal basis. Above all it creates the conditions for the intense intellectual activity associated with modern civilization and thereby creates more favorable conditions for the increase in useful knowledge. In short, urbanization is not only the sole *economical* way to effect industrialization, but in the deeper and perhaps more important sense, it also provides the conditions under which the new way of life can grow and the creative pursuits in art, science, and technology can flourish. These pursuits provide the driving force of the increasing growth potential in the stock of knowledge, and urban life, by spreading them among sufficiently large groups of the population, provides them with a broad base.

NEW PATTERNS OF NATIONAL PRODUCT · The three trends listed above required not only absolutely larger volumes of capital but higher shares of capital formation in national product. A greater rate of increase of population means usually a greater rate of growth of the labor force and, other conditions being equal, a greater rate of additions to capital stock to provide for the increased number of people and workers. Insofar as the rate of growth of total product is raised by the acceleration in the rate of population growth, and the capital coefficients (i.e., ratios of capital to output) remain constant, the proportion of capital formation to national product will rise. Furthermore, the shift in industrial structure meant the setting up of new industries. Many of those, based on the new technology, required large amounts of fixed capital, if only to contain and channel the new powerful sources of energy. And being planned for the long run, the new plants were built before their full capacity could be utilized, which tended to raise the capital-output ratios and to make for higher proportions of capital formation to national product. Finally, urbanization also meant large investments in costly provisions for streets, sanitation, water supply, lighting, transportation, and housing.

It follows that a significant rise in capital formation proportions was requisite for modern economic growth. The statistical records for the early periods of some developed countries, for example Sweden and Denmark, show marked rises in the proportion that net (or gross) additions to capital located within the country formed of net (or gross) domestic or national product. International comparisons at a recent date show that, by and large, these domestic capital formation proportions are much lower in the underdeveloped countries than in the developed countries. For *national* capital formation proportions, which represent the national rate of savings (i.e., domestic adjusted for capital imports or exports), the shift from the low levels of preindustrial times to the higher levels required by modern technology emerges even more sharply.

It may seem at first that the modifications in patterns of use of national product implied by this essential rise in capital formation proportions are moderate and do not involve major changes in economic and social life. After all, the suggested rise is from net capital formation proportions of less than 5 percent to at most about 15 percent, and from gross capital formation proportions of less than 10 percent to about 25 percent. If per capita income rises 10 to 15 percent per decade, as it has in many countries in modern times, keeping per capita consumption unchanged for one decade and adding all of the gain to capital formation would raise the proportions of the latter from 5 to 15 percent. Surely the allocation of a decade's addition to per capita product to capital formation, with no benefit to consumption, does not seem to involve a major social transformation.

But this impression is false for two reasons. The first relates to the timing sequence. If growth of income per capita requires some *antecedent* growth of capital, the rise in the capital formation proportions is needed in advance of the rise in per capita income. To put it more precisely: if a capital formation proportion of 3 percent permitted growth of population at 0.3 percent per year combined with growth in per capita product at 0.1 percent per year, a much larger capital formation proportion will be required just to maintain the per capita product at the same level if population growth is accelerated to 1.0 percent per year. And under such conditions, greater capital accumulation would have to be financed either from abroad or from domestic savings. Financing from abroad, on any sizable scale, might mean some changes at home to permit capital imports on nononerous terms, or special concessions to the foreign creditor that may have distorting or damping effects on economic growth within the country. Financing from domestic savings would mean *reducing* per capita consumption. In other words, the rise in capital formation proportions that must precede any rise in per capita product necessitates substantial changes in the patterns of spending and saving within the country or changes that would induce capital imports from abroad or both.

The second and weightier reason is suggested by the fact that the capital formation proportions are less important than the conditions that give them meaning. In the percentages quoted above, capital formation in the numerator comprised only investments represented by changes in stock of construction, equipment, and inventories (including or excluding net changes in claims against foreign countries as we speak of national or of domestic capital formation). Such capital is effective only if it can be combined with sufficiently skilled labor and management, and developed and underdeveloped countries differ not only in the capital formation proportions but also in the availability of human resources. In this connection, expenditures on some products customarily included under consumer outlay, such as education, recreation, health, and transportation, are capital formation in that they raise the health and skills of labor necessary for combination with material capital. Hence, in emphasizing the rise in capital formation proportions requisite for economic growth, a wider concept of capital is far more relevant, one that would at least include investment in the health and training of the population and in the facilities for social organization that permit increases in productivity. The rises in the capital formation proportions so defined would be far larger than from 5 to 15 percent net, or from 10 to 25 percent gross, and the corresponding international differences between developed and underdeveloped countries would be far wider than those in the ratios currently used. Changes in such proportions would surely mean major shifts in the structure of use of the product and in the patterns of life, and would make the problem of initial capital accumulation all the more complex.

CHANGES IN ECONOMIC ORGANIZATION · Changes in the scale and character of the organizations by which economic activity is carried on are a necessary concomitant of modern technology. The large fixed-capital investments in canals, railroads, steel plants, power stations, and the like could not be entrusted to firms managed by individuals, families, or partnerships. The economic horizon involved far exceeds the life span of an individual or a generation; the mobilization of the necessary savings could not be accomplished without an articulate, nonpersonal structure associated with the limited-liability modern corporation; and the increasing complexity of management requires an organizational form free of the personal limitations of an individual owner or partnership group. Thus the scale of the plant units and the size and life of capital investment required by the technology of modern economic growth, in and of itself, forced a shift from personal ownership-management units to the large-scale corporation. And when the inevitable monopolistic tendencies of the latter, in public utilities, for example, required regulation by the government, regulation in turn contributed to fixing the nonpersonal organization in these industries and at the same time widened the economic role of government, itself a nonpersonal organizational unit.

Empirical data indicate the decline in the shares of capital, product, and labor force engaged under the auspices of individual firms or partnerships, and the increase in the shares controlled by private corporations, and public and governmental bodies, or a mixture of both. The trends are due partly to the rise in relative weight of whole new sectors—railroads, communication, electric light and power, and large-scale manufacturing—which from their beginning had to be nonpersonal organizations, and partly to the increasing share of nonpersonal organizations in sectors where the individual firm or partnership had originally been dominant, such as most manufacturing, construction, trade, and some service industries, and even agriculture. Since both governmental and private corporations are classified as nonpersonal, the suggested trends have only been accelerated by the emergence of the state organization of economic activity exemplified by the USSR.

Three aspects of these trends deserve explicit note. First, the shift required a far-reaching adjustment by members of society. As experience has shown, it is not sufficient to pass a law permitting easy chartering of general purpose, limited-liability corporations.

The people involved, however they are associated with these non-personal organizational units, must act accordingly. A unit that is a publicly chartered, limited-liability corporation in name but is managed as a family firm and so treated by its owners, employees, and the public, is still an individual firm, not a corporation. Governments run by a few families and shot through with nepotism and other forms of corruption are not public agencies but family businesses. Clearly, the growth of genuine nonpersonal organizational units requires a corresponding change in the attitudes of would-be owners, managers, and workers, away from any idea of personal control and relations to rather different and strictly defined roles in these almost statutorily structured units. The owners must learn that their proprietary rights are limited; the managers must learn that they can operate only within specified rules of responsibility and efficiency; and the workers must be ready to accept the purely nonpersonal connection through the labor market.

Second, there is continuous change in the evolution of these nonpersonal organizational units which, when they first emerge, induce these changes in attitudes. Their continued existence strengthens the change and permits further depersonalization of the whole organizational structure. The very increase in the scale of the productive plant and firm forces an increasing distance, as it were, from the direct and personal type of organization: in a plant with only one hundred workers and a few supervisors, personal relations can persist and decisions can be made in a manner that would be dangerous if not impossible in a corporation with thousands of workers and millions of capital investment. On the other hand, the experience gained by people in dealing *via* these nonpersonal organizational units results in a capacity to cooperate that could hardly have been expected of their elders and ancestors, accustomed to entirely different economic relations. The cumulative character of this process and its close interrelation with urbanization and associated changes in patterns of life are particularly to be noted.

Third, the changing relations among owners, managers, workers, and society as a whole play havoc with the older economic theorizing on the subject, much of which survives even today. Perhaps the notable example is the Marxian theory of classes, in which class is related to ownership of means of production, and the class struggle combined with the labor theory of value is used to derive a number of trends in the breakdown of industrial capitalism. In the modern business corporation, the locus of ownership of means of production is vague. Are the owners the thousands of small stockholders, the banks and insurance companies that hold large blocks of stock, on trust as it were, or the managers, who legally are only employees? Is the modern proletariat devoid of control over means of production if a strong union organization can enforce the right to work? What is the role of government in the modern economy? Is it really, as some vulgarized notions of Marxian theory associated with Lenin and his followers claim, a "lackey" of the capitalists, and if so, who are the latter? And is the bureaucracy in the state-controlled economy of the USSR the servant or the master of the people? Why has the "middle" class failed to disappear, and indeed flourished, particularly in countries like the United States where capitalism was most developed? These questions indicate the gap between the oversimplified terminology of the Marxian theory of class struggle and secular transformation of capitalist society and the changes in the structure of economic organization that in fact occurred, partly in connection with the development of the non-personal organizational units in modern economic growth.

CHANGES IN SOCIAL VALUES · The trends in population growth, industrialization, urbanization, spending and saving, and nonpersonal organizational units all imply and must be accompanied by major shifts in the structure of social values. The interplay between social values and the overt processes described by these trends is so close that it is difficult to establish its separate existence. Values are expressed through the behavior of individuals; I cannot point to proofs of the existence of values that are independent of action. Yet it may be argued that modern economic development was partly preceded by and partly accompanied by these shifts in the structure of social values, which had an independent existence in the sense that at critical junctures they constituted the major factor that produced certain social decisions.

The general process of secularization, which placed a high value on the individual and his material welfare in this world instead of his spiritual welfare and the next world, was obviously a foundation without which many trends related to economic growth would have been impossible. This point can be amplified by a few illustrations. The revolution in medicine and public health in England toward the end of the eighteenth century and in the early nineteenth century was not based upon any major scientific discovery. It resulted from a combination of the victory, if only partial, of the empirical frame of mind which refused to accept traditional notions, with a zeal to improve man's lot in this world, a direct rejection of the doctrine of original sin and the view of human suffering as the unavoidable act of a just deity. It is not farfetched to say that this major change in public health practices was largely the result of a change in point of view, in the scale of values. Or to take another example: the theories of human equality, liberty, and fraternity and the denial of the sacredness of status positions not only were instrumental in removing many legal and political obstacles to economic growth but in fact provided the basis upon which the modern view of economic welfare could be developed. And the utilitarian doctrines of the greatest good for the greatest number, which were in a direct line of succession from them, shaped the modern view of social organization and led to the increasing importance of material welfare and economic activity.

This is hardly the place for even a condensed summary of the changes in the view of the world and of mankind that have occurred since the Reformation, the birth of modern science, and the spread of the rationalistic approach. All that need be said here is that, at least as far as Western civilization is concerned—and it is rapidly spreading to the rest of the world—the loss of an overriding religious faith and of the sanctified traditions connected with it not only freed the human mind and effort for the cultivation of science and the arts but also reoriented a vast corpus of human activities. This reorientation was a major prerequisite for modern economic growth. One may regret for esthetic reasons that large proportions of the national product are no longer devoted to pyramids, cathedrals, and castles, but one must admit that power dams, steel furnaces, and skyscrapers are more directly productive of economic growth. One may deplore the decline of those status groups in society that provided for the cultivation of fine traditions, but one must admit that the atomistic, individualistic equality and easy social mobility of modern times are far more conducive to competition and intensive growth. One may lament the lessening of direct contact between man and nature and the desiccation of some values associated with this contact, but one must grant that the complex and abstract system of modern relations is far more efficient, even though it may require acceptance of some tenuous and apparently empty symbols.

Whether we call these views philosophy, theory, mythology, or religion, the point is that they have changed either in advance of, concurrently with, or after the initiation of modern economic growth.

And they *had* to change if such growth was to take place and continue, since the older views were geared to the type of economic and social life that then prevailed. Economic growth, like all processes of social change, is the result of decisions in response to conditions under which some choices exist. And these decisions must be made within the broader framework of theory, mythology, or religion. In the sixteenth and seventeenth centuries an inventor was considered a public nuisance, to be suppressed as a subverter of established order, whereas in our time and country he is considered the motive force of beneficent progress. These different appraisals can only be the expression of different underlying views of the roles of technical progress and business enterprise in attaining desirable goals, and even of the goals themselves. Obviously, such views and appraisals have far-reaching influence on economic growth since they determine decisions by society that set the conditions for economic activity and progress.

THE COST OF TRANSITION · The list of antecedents, concomitants, and consequences of modern economic growth given above could be expanded further. But it is sufficient to suggest the magnitude of the transformation of economic and social life that accompanied modern economic growth and actually formed its substance. We can now appreciate the difficulties and the costs of transition from premodern, preindustrial modes of economic activity and understand why actual economic performance falls short of the potential provided by the increasing stock of useful knowledge.

In considering the problems just suggested, it is useful to distinguish the transition period from the one that follows. The distinction is in a sense artificial: it would be difficult in any specific country's record of economic development to establish the terminal date of the transition period. The process of growth is continuous and at any time in any economy premodern conditions can be found alongside marked changes from old to new. Yet such a distinction helps to separate the period when the bases of modern economic growth were being established and the resistance of the old order was being overcome, from the later period when the self-sustaining and cumulative trends that carry modern economic growth forward emerge.

The historical records provide us with data for several such transition periods: in England from the last quarter of the eighteenth century through the second quarter of the nineteenth century; in the

United States from the 1840's to the 1880's or 1890's with the interruption of the Civil War; in Germany and France from about the middle to the end of the nineteenth century; in Japan from about the late 1870's to about the end of World War I; and finally in Russia from the abortive attempt begun in the 1890's and interrupted by World War I and the Revolution, through the five-year plans of the Soviet regime from the late 1920's to the 1950's. There are also data for the Scandinavian countries, some dominions of the British Empire, and Italy. Each is a case *sui generis*, conditioned by the country's historical heritage and natural endowments, as well as by the particular time and constellation of international conditions associated with it. Yet comparative analysis, which has only been begun, reveals some general features. During the specified periods all these countries show an acceleration in population growth (except in "empty" areas in the New World); a rise in capital formation proportions; a redistribution of population and the labor force, with shifts from agriculture and the countryside to nonagricultural sectors and the cities; changes in the organizational units; and a transformation of values, with high priority given to economic attainment.

These changes do not occur in a vacuum; they are made in societies that usually have a long tradition of the premodern economic organization and social structure, and they must be directed by agents with the power to overcome resistance and incur necessary costs. If agriculture must be changed to permit greater productivity and release labor for other pursuits, the immediate task is to break through the old organizational patterns, to change the relations of man to land, which means in fact dislodging substantial proportions of the population from their accustomed pursuits without disrupting the whole structure of the country's organization and making economic progress impossible. This task was more formidable in the older countries of Western civilization than in its offshoots in the younger and emptier countries. And history is full of the troubles and turmoils when the revolutionary changes took place in the organization and economics of agriculture in England, France, Germany, let alone the USSR during the years of collectivization. The new economics had equally disruptive effects on handicrafts, on small-scale industry and trade, on a variety of established and entrenched sectors of the old economic order, and on the position of the interest groups associated with them.

It is this dislocation and break with the old order that constitutes the major cost of the transition to modern economic growth. Moreover, the benefits of the innovations are not immediate, since it is during this period that the shift to higher proportions of capital formation may occur; and the rise in consumption per capita, if any, must be smaller than the rise in total product per capita. It is during this period also that one mechanism for attaining these results is a wide, perhaps a widening, inequality in the distribution of income—a characteristic not only of the societies that developed under the aegis of the business enterprise but also of those that used the authoritarian power of the state to manage economic processes. Inequality of income in the USSR during the five-year plans was just as great as, if not greater than, in England in the late eighteenth and early nineteenth centuries, and in the United States in the last quarter of the nineteenth century; and such wide inequality puts an extra strain upon the integral framework of any society and requires a special effort to avoid a breakdown that would imperil the whole process.

In short, the transition periods can be described as periods of controlled social and economic revolution. They are revolutions because they involve rapid changes in long-standing economic, social, and often political institutions; they are controlled in that the integrity of the societies is maintained despite prolonged internal conflicts and permits continued cooperation in the rapidly changing economic tasks. Not every society can muster the necessary ingredients: a minority that can assume leadership and an organizational framework and set of values that can hold the population together and make it accept the costs and cooperate with the minority.

The emphasis on the minority is deliberate: it must be a minority since the changes are directed toward the future and cannot represent the immediate interests of the majority which are lodged in the old premodern order. This minority may be the emerging groups of industrialists and modern agriculturists, the intellectual propagandists of the new order recruited from the educated groups, or some political party that craves power and is willing to force an industrialization program through in order to consolidate its leadership and raise the economic power of the state under its control. But this innovating minority must have minimum cooperation from the population, and it may secure it by different means, ranging from authoritarian compulsion backed by powerful propaganda to instill allegiance to the "wave of the future," to a laissez-faire attitude with government setting the permissive conditions by removing obstacles and providing encouragement on the theory that the activities of the private entrepreneurial groups will redound to the benefit of society as a whole.

The interplay between private groups and the state machinery in this transition process is at the core of much recent controversy. I am not competent to deal with it, nor can we treat it with sufficient detail here. But the interpretation of the historical record has been vulgarized by propagandistic mythology, and two resulting errors should be rejected. The first is the notion that the state played only a passive minimal role in the transition periods of capitalist societies. The most cursory reference to the record dispels this illusion. Even in the United States, which was perhaps as free as any country from the binding historical heritage that requires forcible removal by state power, the record is full of decisions by the state on matters that were vital to economic growth, where a different set of decisions would have meant a different course of economic growth. Every decade marked some decision by the state —on currency, on tariffs, on internal improvements, on land, on labor, on immigration—and each one was reached after explicit discussion in which its importance for the country's economic growth was recognized. This active role of the state was even more patent in the older countries, where the state had to decide about the abolition of old rights and the introduction of new. And this is inevitable: insofar as economic growth necessitates shifts in position, it is a source of internal conflict which can be resolved only by the power of the sovereign state. This is essentially what the state organization is for.

The second error is the opposite of the first: that since the government represents a single organized entity, the state can, by planning and managing, attain a speedier and more effective transition to the new economic order than if the major role were left to private enterprise. Given the past historical record of transition during which private enterprise did play an important part, with much turmoil and suffering, this preference for the orderly and planned performance by the state seems attractive. But it is an illusion. For economic development, and the transition to the new order, is a costly process no matter who guides it, and there is no assurance that the costs will be smaller if the guide is an authoritarian state, essentially an entrenched minority, rather than a democratic state responsive to the pressures of organized groups that represent different interests. The contrast is not between a guided and unguided period of transition or between a planned and unplanned process of economic development. It is rather between guidance by a democratically organized government and guidance by a dictatorship of some minority party; between a plan that reflects some broad theory of economic development subject to change and is put into action *via* some broad secular decisions by government, and a plan that is a compendium of specific priorities and targets compiled by the minority that runs the state machinery in accordance with policy decisions that have not benefited from free discussion.

There are obviously various combinations of democracy and authoritarianism in the use of governmental machinery and private enterprise in the transition process. The relative advantages and disadvantages have to be weighed in terms of the specific character of the combination, the specific conditions, and priorities to be assigned to the short run versus the long run. But on the face of it, one could reasonably argue that if economic growth and development are essentially for the benefit of the members of society, and if they also have to sustain the costs, the broadest participation in decisions by governments that bear upon economic growth is probably the best assurance of maximizing returns and minimizing costs. Granted that continued education of the majority to help it adjust to changing conditions and to make for more farsighted and intelligent decisions is needed, it still seems wiser to require that the minorities, with their articulate views of possible and desirable courses of economic growth, secure approval of their programs from the majorities within a democratic framework, rather than give them the right and power to force the programs on the population. And one need not go too far into the historical records of the authoritarian states to conclude that the cost of the economic transition that they accomplished was extremely high in terms of human lives, while considerable doubt remains whether the results warrant optimism for further economic growth. This naturally is an impression, but whether or not one accepts it, the point to be stressed is that the very nature of the transition period involves a major role of government and state machinery.

These are surely sparse comments on a large problem. But although much more could have been said, the comparative analysis of the transition periods in the twelve to eighteen countries is still to be made, and further discussion of this topic depends upon the results of this analysis.

SUSTAINING GROWTH AFTER THE TRANSITION · How is the pace of economic growth sustained after the transition period? Two points might give this question more substance. First, there have been notable differences in the rates of growth among all the countries that have shifted from the preindustrial to the modern economic basis. Second, even apparently minor differences in the rates of growth sustained over a long period cumulate into large differences. A per capita income that rises 1 percent per year reaches about 164 percent of its original level in 50 years; one that rises 1.5 percent per year is 211 percent of its initial level in 50 years.

The reasons for sustained growth after the transition period are clear enough: the accumulation of capital, both material and invested in the skills and health of the population; the transformation of economic and social institutions; the changed patterns of population growth; and the changed scale of values all permit continued and increasing exploitation of the stock of useful knowledge, and the latter is continuously growing. If some rates of economic growth are appreciably below others, or if some diminish rapidly from the high levels reached at the end of the transition period, the transformation to modern economic processes must have been incomplete or the adaptation of economic and social institutions must have encountered increasingly formidable difficulties.

In this connection the heritage of the transition period may be important, for the ways in which some problems are resolved will determine the capacity of the economy to adapt itself further to the increasing potential of economic growth. The historical record is full of instances where the adjustments in the transition process have been a source of difficulty in generating and sustaining a high rate of growth. In the United States, the resolution of difficulties by the Civil War set a basis for the vigorous economic growth that followed, but the effects of slavery in the South were never fully removed and because of persisting race discrimination policies, the South remained backward and in a way acted as a brake upon the rate of economic growth of the country as a whole. In Germany, the privileged position granted to some land-owning groups, particularly in East Prussia, in order to lower their resistance to the new economic order, remained an element of distortion in the economic and social structure that was productive of later troubles, internal and external. Such evidence of incomplete transition can be identified in almost every country, even if its effects on the rate of economic growth cannot be measured.

These elements of the old economic and social order that may persist during the process of transition are not the only obstacles to the maintenance of a high rate of economic growth. The very changes made in transition may set up entrenched interests and positions which, with changing conditions, become foci of resistance to further changes and hence to further growth. A notable example is the evolution of large-scale firms to monopolistic or near-monopolistic dimensions, with the power to limit competition and perhaps to retard the rate of growth. And we are witnessing right now in the USSR an attempt to reduce the consequences of restrictive elements in the dictatorial organization of the country, to minimize the prestige of the Stalinist regime in its authoritarian and ruthless aspects. No hard and fast generalizations can be drawn, except that high rates of growth mean rapid changes in structure, and any factors that make for the entrenchment of those interests which may be displaced in the process of structural change will thereby set up obstacles to a high rate of economic progress.

It is this circumstance that heightens the importance of the impulses to growth that result from additions to the stock of useful knowledge and from the capacity of society for social invention and innovation. The strategic property of technological changes is that they provide avenues for further growth in new areas of supply and demand not directly limited by the old entrenched interests. Competition and progress within the railroad sector may be stifled by its monopolistic character. But it will be vigorous in the general field of transportation services if technological changes create new opportunities, for example in air and truck transportation. And such interindustry competition may revitalize the railroads themselves. The possibilities of growth in the cotton-textile industry may be limited because only slight further reductions of costs are feasible regardless of technological changes. But if invention yields a new product with comparable uses, such as rayon or nylon, the growth potential increases and may sustain the rate of increase in all the textile industries as a whole. In other words, although at any given time the existing stock of knowledge is not fully utilized, the additions to it open up new areas in which the obstacles are less formidable than in the old. In that sense a continuous flow of inventions and innovations is indispensable if a high rate of economic growth is to be sustained.

Equally indispensable is the capacity of society to devise and accept the institutional changes that may be necessary for these changes in technology and substance of economic production. The introduction of the automobile was surely a major element in sustaining economic growth in the United States after World War I, but the integration of this vast new industry and its subsidiaries needed more than the new plants and new skills. It required institutional adjustments, for example the development of financial institutions to make installment selling possible and economical and thus overcome the difficulties involved in financing this high-cost, durable commodity out of current consumer income. It also required a network of roads that had to be built, managed, and financed—functions new to the existing governmental institutions.

A study of the social, political, and economic institutions of a country and of the methods by which they adjust to the changing opportunities for economic growth provided by new products, new tools, new materials, and new industries would be a difficult but highly rewarding task. The process goes far beyond the simple conception of a Schumpeterian entrepreneur developing an innovation despite the resistance of the mass of the population. The capacity for change is widespread, as is resistance to it. There are elements of both in the functioning of social institutions and in the activities of the human beings who are the carriers of economic and social life. The willingness to experiment with change differs from country to country and period to period. But it is beyond my competence to suggest more precisely how institutional patterns in the organization of society could be analyzed in order to test this capacity for change which is clearly an indispensable prerequisite of a sustained high rate of economic growth.

International Relations and Economic Growth

The economic growth of a country is affected by its coexistence with many other countries, and we supplement our reflections on the *internal* adjustment of a nation to the economic-growth potential by comments on the bearing of *international* relations. Much of modern economic growth is incomprehensible unless it is seen as a reflection of strains and pressures imposed upon a nation by membership in the worldwide concert of nation-states. Hence, although our com-

ments will again be necessarily sketchy, they should serve to emphasize some broad points.

We begin with the following characteristics of nations, as we
use the term here: the presence of sovereign state power, which
is indispensable for making overriding decisions that set the conditions of economic growth (the function that makes the nation the
necessary unit in the study of economic growth); the exercise of this
power over a social group located in a specified area, which gives
meaning to the terms "territory" and "territorial boundaries"; and
possession by that group of a common history, in the sense that its
members have a feeling of cohesion and as a group have experienced events that are their particular heritage. Their past may have
stretched over centuries or over decades, but the sharing of this
common historical past is indispensable to the feeling of cohesion
which is the basis upon which the internal power of the sovereign
state rests.

On the meaning of these characteristics there have been long
and voluminous disputes. The sovereign power of the state vis-à-vis
other organizations within the country has been the subject of
much discussion, and the internal limits of sovereignty have been a
topic of cautious speculation in political theory. Territory has also
been a matter of disputatious definition, not only in specific con-
troversies over boundaries but also in connection with problems that
emerge whenever man reaches out into another aspect of the
universe. Air travel has led to new questions of sovereignty over
the air, and the prospective development of satellites may upset
many current legal notions concerning national boundaries. History
is written and rewritten, and the common history of a group in the
viewpoint of some members of a nation may be considered the
record of an oppressive and "foreign" majority by some dissident
splinter group. But we need not be concerned with the finer points
if the three characteristics are taken in their broader meaning as
necessary and sufficient to distinguish the nation-state as a unit
for which economic growth is studied and among several of which
there exist what we call international relations.

From these characteristics we can derive the general nature of
international relations, particularly those with economic substance.
Nations necessarily differ with respect to territory, since sovereignty
is overriding and impenetrable and only one power, in the modern
political structure of nations, can reign over one territory. The
several segments of the earth, with their different locations, will

have different climatic and topographical characteristics and different supplies of natural resources. The possession of a common history means, *ipso facto*, possession of a past different from that of any other group, even if the two groups are close to each other and participate in many common occurrences. A distinctive history ordinarily means also a distinctive constellation of economic and social resources, as a reflection of different scales of values and traditions. Hence not only natural but historical conditions make for differences among nations in economic performance, thus allowing for comparative advantages in international trade, for various pushes and pulls in international migration, and for differences in the attraction of capital in its international movement. Furthermore, since a major purpose of the sovereign state is to secure the country's "place in the sun," there is considerable opportunity for conflicts, for the exercise of political power may run from a mild negotiated arrangement like securing trading rights with other countries to a major intervention like assuming sovereignty over another area and its inhabitants as a colony. The network of international relations is thus partly a web of peaceful, economically motivated flows of goods, men, and capital and partly a web of pressures and tensions that alternate between periods of warless equilibrium and displacement and periods of overt conflicts.

Although the source of economic growth in the stock of useful knowledge is largely transnational, its application—the actual process of economic growth—is most unequal. The transition to the modern level of economic performance occurred in some nations before it did in others, and consequently at any given time some nations were at higher economic levels than others and some nations were growing more rapidly than others.

The unequal impact of economic growth upon nations was due largely to differences in historical background and antecedents. Thus when modern science developed and knowledge reached a point where an industrial revolution could take place, some nations were ready for it but others were not. Were one to ask in what country in the second half of the eighteenth century one could have expected the Industrial Revolution—in the sense of a complex of new methods of agricultural production, new industrial materials in the form of iron and steel (or an approximation to the latter like bar iron), and a new source of power in the form of steam—the answer is that only a few countries felt the need for these new methods of production, and only a few countries could muster the capacity to adapt their economic and social institutions to a wide-scale application of these inventions and discoveries. It was no accident that the Industrial Revolution occurred in England in the second half of the eighteenth century. It was no accident that the countries on the western and northern periphery of Europe— Spain, Portugal, France, the Netherlands, and England—were most active and in fact pioneered in the geographical revolution that led to the discovery of the New World and ushered in the long period of economic growth associated with merchant capitalism.

The major innovation, if one can call it that, which is the base and substance of a distinct epoch in economic growth, does not occur simultaneously in all the nations that comprise mankind, but unfolds itself in a long sequence, beginning in one or two nations which are the pioneering units and spreading to others. This spread of the industrial system, which is the essential substance of economic growth of nations during the period under discussion, points immediately to the significance of international relations. They helped to spread the impetus and basis of economic growth from their point of origin in the pioneering country to the followers, early or late, and thus to domination of economic activity the world over.

No specific attention will be paid in this paper to the long-term movements in peace-type international flows of goods and services in the current transactions accounts, of men in international migration, and of short- or long-term capital funds. These are fairly well-known, and their influence in spreading economic growth can be easily perceived. The increasing extent to which the countries that were earliest to adopt the industrial system of economic production exported the new products and thus the new tastes and techniques—aided by revolutionary changes in means of transportation and communication and by the provision for capital credits— needs no emphasis. It is also clear that the expanding international migration, in the nineteenth and early twentieth centuries, which was voluntary and not politically compulsory, often meant the importation of advanced technological skills and, in any case, helped to man the most promising opportunities for economic growth. The intriguing aspect of these peace-type international flows is the political or power element implicit in them, which grew in importance to a point of forcing a sharp reversal in trend about the time of World War I. This brings us immediately to the political or power element of international relations, which, at its height, results in the use of overt force in armed conflict.

By political or power element I mean simply the threat, implicit

or explicit, of the use of physical sanctions. Any action backed by
such a threat, whether in offense or defense, is a political or power
action. In this meaning, the element is indispensable to the whole
concept of a sovereign nation-state. If several million Ruritanians
set up their own government and declare their right to govern
themselves, they are telling the Lusitanians, Aquitanians, and
other inhabitants of the world that they are ready to defend by
physical force the right to pass their own laws and enforce these
laws upon their fellow Ruritanians. And the sovereign state must
retain the monopoly of major physical sanctions within the country no matter how many other rights and privileges it is willing to
share with other organizations.

We stress this point because there must be an inescapable power
element in all international relations, insofar as they are relations
among sovereign states or citizens of states, and if there is, trends
in the extent to which it affects international relations are important
in their bearing upon economic growth of nations. Thus trading
in commodities between the members of two sovereign states, under
the prevalent theory and practice of sovereign states, *may* be a
matter of easily enforceable agreement; but it may be impossible
unless one of the states exercises power pressure to force the other
to permit trading—as has happened repeatedly in the last century
between some Western power and some country in Asia or Africa.
And what is true of commodity trade is true of international migration and of international movements of capital.

The threat of force in international relations is so widespread,
particularly in relations between countries at widely different levels
of economic development and with different historical heritage and
traditions, that it is not easy to measure its use or effects on international relations within the last two centuries. It can range from
what may seem to be enforcement of the most elementary requirement of decent intercourse to ruthless subjugation of another state.
Overt conflicts are only part of the story. A threat of force that does
not result in war because one party yields is still use of force and
represents a political or power element in the relation established.
Nevertheless, two fairly broad conclusions can be suggested as
tentative hypotheses. First, this use of force, this political or power
element in international relations, is an important mechanism in
the spread of economic growth. Second, its relative weight in international relations, and *pari passu* in spreading economic growth,
has increased in the recent half to three quarters of a century.

The first hypothesis can be reduced to a simple paradigm. There will be no continuous economic relations between two countries at different stages of economic and social development unless the more advanced country forces upon the less advanced some conditions that permit stable trade and other relations. The plausibility of this thesis is apparent when one considers that the legal and social framework of any society is closely interrelated with its economic activity and conditions. Differences in economic and social levels therefore make agreement upon conditions of intercourse difficult, and the difficulty is likely to be overcome by the pressure of the economically advanced and hence more powerful nation. Without continuous economic relations between the "laggard" and the more advanced countries, the drive toward modern economic growth is not likely to be generated in the former. It follows that the "opening up" of the laggard countries by the threat of force on the part of the advanced countries is a prerequisite for the spread of economic growth to the former.

This pattern seems simple enough, but it is true only for countries at widely different levels of economic and social development and hence of power. It finds classic corroboration in the "opening up" of Japan and the spread of modern economic growth to that country. It is also an apt description of the effects of Western aggression in many other countries of Asia and Africa. But what about the spread of the industrial system within Europe proper or to the United States? Was any power element instrumental in spreading modern economic growth to these areas from its original locus in Great Britain? The answer is obvious since the power or force element can be used defensively as well as offensively. The sovereign power in the United States and in many European countries was exercised to limit the economic activities of a more advanced country and thus provide more favorable conditions for domestic industrialization. It was no accident that the theory of protection originated in the United States and spread to Germany, and that the United States utilized its sovereign power in its war for independence late in the eighteenth century to set up conditions for rapid economic growth in the nineteenth century.

The heart of the matter is that the political power of the sovereign state is almost indispensable. It is used to mobilize energies within a country for the purpose of economic growth despite the risks and burdens, or to extend the sway of sovereignty into other areas. In either case, it helps spread the new system of economic production as it did in earlier eras. The dominant power organization of society must be involved in the extension of any new methods of economic production, particularly if they necessitate rapid and thoroughgoing transformations such as those associated with the modern industrial system.

I do not mean to argue that the power element in the organization of the sovereign state is always favorable to the spread of economic growth. It sometimes is used to retard it, to isolate a society from the virus of economic change. But on balance the contribution of the power element in international relations is positive simply because it is also a function of economic growth. Despite the disruption, exploitation, and harm that aggression by Western powers brought to preindustrial Asia, Africa, and Latin America, the record of economic growth already achieved in these areas and foreseeable in the future is probably far richer than if they had remained in complete isolation. Despite the costs and wastes of tariffs, protection, and the like, the industrialization and economic growth of countries like the United States and Germany probably exceed the levels that could have been reached with completely free international trade. This does not mean automatic justification of possible excesses in the use of political power, internally or externally, but only recognition of the indispensability of some political power for economic growth. One may well deplore the use of force by a sovereign state for external compulsion or for artificial isolation in international relations, but if the primary concern is with the rise of over-all product, total or per capita, without considering cost and welfare implications, the use of force in international relations does in the long run accelerate the spread of modern economic growth to increasing numbers of nations.

The conclusion that the use of force in international relations has grown in recent decades is an impression, but there are many straws pointing in this direction. The last four decades have witnessed two widespread and relatively costly world wars. What might be called the "politicization" of the peace-type flows—commodity trade, international migration, capital imports and exports—has become more pronounced since World War I; that is, the elements in these flows motivated by political interests of state have become proportionately greater. In several countries, which account for a substantial proportion of world population, the control of the dictatorial state apparatus over international relations is so tight that relations with other national units are essentially a monopoly of the government. All these changes constitute the substance of the long-term trend suggested. But more important are the reasons behind them since they throw some light on the nature of economic growth of nations in the modern or even earlier epochs. Insofar as one can see, and it is only a speculative suggestion, the increased tension and force in international relations were due to the spread of the new system of economic production, to the emergence of several advanced countries, and to the pressures and struggles that resulted therefrom. The revival of imperialism came only in the last quarter of the nineteenth century, when the United States and Germany emerged as industrial powers threatening the supreme position of Great Britain. The addition of Japan and later of Russia to the roll only increased the possibilities of friction in the struggle for position.

Three features of this spread of economic growth to several major nations deserve note. First, the later a country enters the transition phase from the preindustrial to the industrial system, the greater its lag—for more time has elapsed and the leaders have had a greater opportunity to enjoy the cumulative advantage of greater growth. Given the existing power relations, this sets up increasing tension in the laggard countries and makes the leaders of their industrialization process anxious for quick results to assure them of the minimum economic power necessary to preserve internal stability and external independence. The elements of haste and pressure in the industrialization of Japan and the USSR can be viewed in part as results of fear, warranted or unwarranted, that any delay in reducing the lag would threaten their security.

Second, the correlation between the time span of the lag and the differences in historical heritage and conditions between the pioneer countries and the followers, while not perfect, is significant. The latest countries in the industrialization process—Japan, the USSR, and most recently China—are less like England than the earlier followers, the United States and Germany. The social and political conditions that had to be adapted to the new industrial system were also different, and although certain changes had to be made in them, there was nevertheless room and need for some other political and social concomitants. It is significant that the element of authoritarianism and direct state intervention increases progressively as the time lag in industrialization grows, a product partly of the increasing strain of backwardness and partly of the political and historical heritage within which the modern economic process has to be fitted.

Third, since the emergence of new economic leaders weakens the power of the old, there tends to be a dissolution of some old international relations and the formation of new sovereign nation-states. This readjustment of the political framework to changed power relations sometimes requires a prolonged armed conflict as a final test, but may often take place without a major war. Since the early twentieth century, several such dissolutions have taken place and new sovereign states have emerged, the heirs of the Turkish, Austro-Hungarian, and recently the British and French empires. The process is continuing and the number of independent nation-states is increasing apace.

One result of the spread of the industrial system to an increasing number of nations, of the intensification of the spirit of nationalism which strengthens the power element of the sovereign state, and of the multiplication of nation-states amid increasing tension has been the proliferation of various types of international relations and of political and social organizations designed for economic growth. It may be that the international flows exemplified by lend-lease, Marshall Plan aid, and Point Four are not new. In the long course of social history there may have been many such subventions and aids, but these forms of international flows have not been usual in the peacetime decades of the last two centuries. International agencies and their economic activities may have had their parallels in an earlier past, but they are certainly a recent development in the history of the last two centuries.

The same can be said of the political and social organizations that have been devised, and apparently are going to be devised, for the purpose of exploiting the economic growth potential of the stock of useful knowledge. Some social concomitants of the industrial system are indispensable. However, they still allow for a variety of combinations of the state and private groups, and the patterns that will emerge in countries still to be industrialized cannot be expected to be replicas of those already established. This variety of growth organization and experience, past and prospective, is to some extent an inevitable consequence of the variety of historical heritages and antecedents that shape the characteristics of the scores of nations which, for reasons indicated, must rely on the powers of their sovereign governments to assist them in the transition to the modern economic system.

The Importance of "Noneconomic" Factors

This discussion has purposely underemphasized the economic aspects of economic growth. Much more could have been said about